MASTERING NEW YORK'S GRADE 8 ENGLISH LANGUAGE ARTS STANDARDS

MARK JARRETT

STUART ZIMMER

JAMES KILLORAN

JARRETT PUBLISHING COMPANY

EAST COAST OFFICE
P.O. Box 1460
Ronkonkoma, NY 11779
631-981-4248

SOUTHERN OFFICE
60 Nettles Boulevard
Jensen Beach, FL 34957
800-859-7679

WEST COAST OFFICE
10 Folin Lane
Lafayette, CA 94549
925-906-9742

1-800-859-7679   Fax: 631-588-4722
www.jarrettpub.com

Grateful acknowledgment is made to the following to reprint the copyrighted materials listed below:

Address delivered to the World Social Forum in January, 2005, "From Justice to Democracy By Way of the Bells" by José Saramago of Portugal. *Ask Magazine*, "What Killed the Dinosaurs," by Dana MacKenzie in the November 2005 issue. August House Publishers for "The Lion's Whiskers," by Pleasant DeSpain from *Thirty-Three Multi-Cultural Tales To Tell*, © 1993. Berkley Publishing Group, *It's Not about the Bike: My Journey Back to Life* by Lance Armstrong, © 2001. Black Dog and Leventhal Publishers, Inc. for "The Gift of the Magi" by O. Henry in *One Hundred and One Read-Aloud Classics,* edited by Pamela Horn, © 1995. Cobblestone Publishing for the articles in *Cobblestone Magazine*, "The House That Jane Built" by Shawn Hoffelt, © 1994; and "El Camino Real" by Robert J. Torrez, © 1998. Congdon and Weed, Inc., for *Growing Up* by Russell Baker, © 1982. Delacorte Press for "The Grass" and "Morning" by Emily Dickinson from *Favorite Poems: Old and New*, Helen Ferris, editor, © 1957. Dover Publications, Inc., for "The Piece of String" by Guy de Maupassant, from *The Necklace and Other Short Stories*, © 1992. Groundwood Books for *The Breadwinner* by Deborah Ellis, © 2000. Health Communications, Inc. for "A Good Reason to Look Up" by Shaquille O'Neal, from *Chicken Soup for the Kid's Soul*, ed. by Canfield, J., Hansen, M.V., Hansen, P., and Dunlap, I., © 1998. *Highlights For Children* for "Marian's Revolution" by Sudipta Bardhan-Quallen, January, 2001 issue; for "Seeing Through Dorothea's Eyes" by Sudipta Bardhan, April, 2005 issue. Henry Holt and Co. for "The Road Not Taken" by Robert Frost, from *Mountain Interval*, © 1920. Junior Scholastic for "The New Immigrants" by Naomi Marcus, September, 1998, Volume 101, Number 2, in *Junior Scholastic Magazine* © 1998. *National Geographic*, "Orangutans Hanging Tough," by Dr. Cheryl Knott in the October, 2003 issue. *Poetry Magazine* for "Flower-fed Buffaloes" by Vachel Lindsay, © 1913. Putnam Publishing Group for "Mei-Jing And Her Piano," from *The Joy Luck Club* by Amy Tan, © 1989. Random House for "We're All In The Phone Book" by Langston Hughes in *The Collected Poems of Langston Hughes*, edited by Arnold Rampersaud © 1995. Random House for "How Reading Changed My Life" by Anna Quindlen, © 1998. Simon and Schuster for "The Hero of Indian Cliff" adapted from C.H. Claudy, *The Children's Book of Heroes*, by William J. Bennett, editor, © 1997. Simon and Schuster for "The Bridge Builder" by Will Allen Dromgoole, "The Story of Scarface," and "The Bell of Atri" as retold by James Baldwin, from *The Book of Virtues For Young People,* William J. Bennett, editor, © 1997. *New York Times* for "Synchronizing the Present and Past in a Timeless Place, © September 12, 2005. Viking-Penguin Books for "The Grapes of Wrath," by John Steinbeck, © 1939. NOTE*: In some cases the previously published material has been adapted and edited to maintain an eighth grade readability level.*

ACKNOWLEDGMENTS

The authors would like to thank the following educators who helped review the manuscript. Their comments, suggestions, and recommendations have proved invaluable in preparing this book.

Linda Smolen
Director of Reading, Buffalo Public Schools
Buffalo School District

Ann Herz
West Lake Middle School
Mt. Pleasant School District

Cover design, layout, graphics, and typesetting: Burmar Technical Corporation, Albertson, N.Y.

This book is dedicated…

to my wife, Gośka, and my children Alexander and Julia — *Mark Jarrett*

to my wife Joan, my children Todd and Ronald, and my grandchildren Katie and Jared — *Stuart Zimmer*

to my wife Donna, my children Christian, Carrie, and Jesse, and my grandchildren Aiden, Christian, and Olivia — *James Killoran*

Also by Killoran, Zimmer, and Jarrett

Mastering New York's Grade 3 English Language Arts Standards
Mastering New York's Grade 4 English Language Arts Standards
Mastering New York's Grade 5 English Language Arts Standards
Mastering New York's Grade 4 English Language Arts Test
Mastering New York's Grade 8 English Language Arts Test
Introducing the Elementary English Language Arts
Mastering the Elementary English Language Arts
Mastering the MCAS Grade 3 Reading Test
Mastering the Grade 4 MCAS Test in English Language Arts
Mastering the Grade 3 FCAT in Reading
Mastering the Grade 4 FCAT in Reading
Excelling on the Grade 10 FCAT in Reading
Mastering the TAKS Grade 3 in Reading
Mastering the TAKS Grade 4 in Reading and Writing
Mastering the TAKS Grade 5 in Reading
Mastering the TAKS Grade 7 Writing TEKS
Mastering the TAKS Grade 11 Exit Level ELA
Mastering the Grade 5 PSSA Reading Test
Mastering the Grade 6 PSSA Writing Assessment
Mastering the Grade 3 ISAT Reading and Writing Test
Mastering the Grade 5 ISAT Reading and Writing Test
Mastering Ohio's Fourth Grade Proficiency Tests in Reading and Writing
Mastering the Georgia Middle Grades Writing Assessment
La Prepa: Dominando la prueba TAKS de lectura de 3er grado

TABLE OF CONTENTS

WHAT LIES AHEAD

This year, you will take the **Grade 8 English Language Arts Test**. This test consists of three sessions. *Session 1*, lasting 45 minutes, focuses on your reading skills. You will be given four or five literary and informational passages, and will have to answer 26 multiple-choice questions about what you have read. *Session 2* will also last 45 minutes. During this session, you will listen to an informational passage read aloud two times. You will then be asked to answer one extended-response and three short-response questions about the listening passage. *Session 3*, lasting 60 minutes, is based on two paired passages — one literary and one informational. You will read the passages and answer one extended-response and three short-response questions.

Mastering New York's Grade 8 English Language Arts Standards has two purposes. First, this book will help you to improve your reading, listening, and writing skills. Second, this book will help you to perform your very best on the **Grade 8 English Language Arts Test**. A brief summary of each unit will explain how this book can help you to improve your skills and prepare you for the test.

INTRODUCTION

The introductory unit consists of three chapters. The first chapter reviews the key strategies of good readers. The second and third chapters review the basic elements of literary and informational texts. You will learn about the setting, characters, plot and theme of a story; the characteristics of poetry; and how to identify the main idea and supporting details in an informational text.

SESSION 1: READING

The main part of this book consists of three units — each one named after one of the three "sessions" of the **Grade 8 English Language Arts Test**. The first of these units, "Session 1: Reading," presents a series of chapters organized by different reading comprehension skills. These same comprehension skills also form the basis for the different types of questions that will appear on the test. In this unit, you will learn how to apply decoding strategies to figure out the meaning of unfamiliar words; how to grasp the meaning of a reading as a whole; how to locate individual details and relate those details to one another (such as by sequence, cause and effect or comparing-and-contrasting); how to analyze the elements of a story; and how to go beyond a basic understanding of a reading by making predictions or drawing conclusions.

You will also learn how to answer questions about an author's use of literary techniques, and about the reliability of the information found in an informational text. This unit concludes with a diagnostic **Session 1 Practice Test** with the same kinds of readings and multiple-choice questions found on the actual test. A concept map on page 204 summerizes the skills in this unit.

SESSION 2: LISTENING AND WRITING

This unit prepares you for **Session 2** of the test. The first chapter shows you how to improve your listening and note-taking skills. Helpful hints are provided for a variety of note-taking formats. The next chapter explores the ways short-response questions might be asked and how to write a response. You will also learn how to answer questions asking you to complete a web, sequence map, or chart. The last chapter of the unit looks at how to answer extended-response questions. Here you will review student responses to an extended-response question and score them to see what needs to be included for a high-scoring response. You will also learn about the key elements of good writing: *meaning*, *organization*, *development*, *language use*, and *conventions*.

SESSION 3: READING AND WRITING

In this unit, you will learn how to analyze paired passages and how to answer questions about them. This is followed by a chapter in which you will practice writing both short and extended responses based on linked passages.

A FINAL PRACTICE TEST

The book concludes with a complete practice **Grade 8 English Language Arts Test**, accurately reflecting the number of questions and the level of difficulty of the actual test. This practice test will help you and your teacher focus on any remaining weaknesses that might still need to be addressed. This practice test is followed by an *Appendix* with the most important rules for good writing mechanics.

By paying careful attention to your teacher and by using this book as your guide, you can be confident that you will do your best on the day the actual test is given. Good luck with the Grade 8 English Language Arts Test!

INTRODUCTION

The opening unit of this book will teach you how to become a better reader.

⭐ In **Chapter 1**, you will learn the strategies that good readers often use to better understand what they read.

⭐ There are several types of selections you should be able to read. **Chapter 2** looks at the elements of literary texts, such as stories, including their setting, characters, plot and theme. This chapter also looks at the special characteristics of poetry.

⭐ **Chapter 3** looks at the parts of informational readings, including the main idea and supporting details.

CHAPTER 1

THE STRATEGIES OF GOOD READERS

The **Grade 8 English Language Arts Test** consists of three important building blocks essential for thinking and communicating: reading, listening, and writing. This introductory chapter looks more closely at the first of these related processes.

THE PROCESS OF READING

A large part of the **Grade 8 English Language Arts Test** will test your ability to read. But what exactly does it mean to "read" something? Although you have been reading since the first grade, have you ever stopped to think what a complex process reading really is?

Describe what you do when you "read" something.

_____

_____

_____

_____

_____

When you read, you look at letters on a page. From those letters, your brain forms words. Next, your brain puts these words together to make up meaningful ideas. The process of reading is therefore one of making up — or constructing — **meaning** from a text. Understanding the writer's ideas is the most important part of reading.

THE IMPORTANCE
OF BACKGROUND KNOWLEDGE

You often use your own knowledge and experience to make sense out of the words on a page. Your background knowledge therefore plays an essential role in the process of reading. To better illustrate this point, read the following paragraph:

> Rocky slowly lifted himself up, planning his escape. What he disliked most was being held. He carefully considered his present position. The lock that held him was powerful, but he thought he could break it. He realized, however, that he would have to carry out his attempt without error.
>
> *In your own words, describe what is happening in the passage:*
>
> _____
> _____
> _____
> _____
> _____
> _____

What did you think the passage was about? When this reading was given to college students studying music, they concluded it was about a jail break. However, when the identical passage was read by students studying physical education, they concluded it was about wrestling. If you carefully reread the words of the passage, you will see that it could really be about either situation. The author does not exactly explain where or how Rocky was held. The background knowledge of the reader must fill in the "gaps" left by the writer.

As you can see, background knowledge is crucial to your understanding of a written text. There are always "gaps" in a text that the reader must fill in. Background knowledge helps you to make sense, or to construct meaning, out of the words of a text. It is therefore very important to stay alert and think about the text as you read. Your own knowledge and experience will shape how you see and interpret what you read.

KEY READING STRATEGIES

Now that you have considered what the process of reading is, let's look at how to become a better reader. Experts in reading have identified several strategies used by good readers to better understand and make sense of what they read. These include things that good readers do *before*, *during* and *after* reading any passage.

BEFORE READING

When you are about to read something, you should always ask yourself:

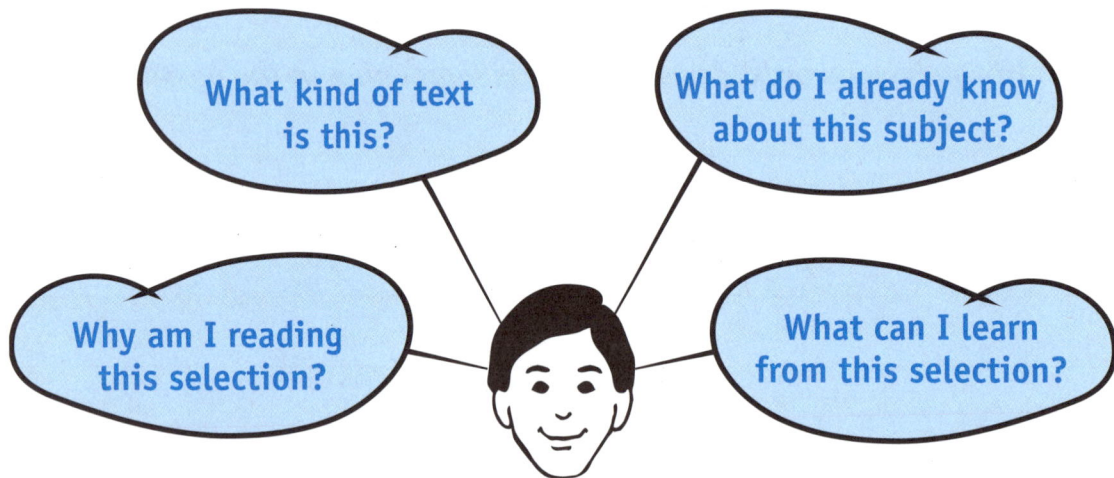

What kind of text is this?

What do I already know about this subject?

Why am I reading this selection?

What can I learn from this selection?

Think about **why** you are reading the selection. Is it to find out information, to enjoy a good story, or for some other reason? Your purpose for reading will help determine **how** you read. For example, will you just try to picture mentally what is happening in the passage, or should you take detailed notes to record specific information?

Next, look over the title and the rest of the selection to get a general idea of what it is about. See if there are illustrations, subheadings, or other clues about the subject of the reading. Then think about what you already know about this kind of text and its subject.

The type of text will often affect how you read:

★ If the selection is *literary*, first think about the setting and the characters. Where does the story take place? Who is it about? What are their problems?

★ If the selection is *informational*, ask yourself what you already know about that topic. Then think what you might want to learn from the selection.

DURING READING

Good readers think actively as they read. It is almost like they are having a little conversation with the text in their heads. You can also do this in the following ways:

ASK YOURSELF QUESTIONS

As you read, ask yourself questions about what you are reading. For example, good readers ask *where* and *when* the action takes place. Good readers ask *what* is happening in the reading. They also ask *why* things in the story happen the way they do. This is one of the most important parts of reading. Asking yourself questions helps you to stay focused on what you are reading.

MAKE CONNECTIONS

As you read, ask yourself if what you are reading reminds you of anything you already know. This could be something that you experienced in your own life or something you have read or heard about. Then compare what the reading says to what you already know. See if what you read adds to your knowledge or changes your way of thinking. For example, if you are reading a story, do the characters remind you of real people? If you are reading a description of a real event, does it remind you of any situation you have ever experienced yourself?

THINK ABOUT WHAT IS IMPORTANT

As you read, focus on the author's *main ideas* or the *key events* in the story. Ask yourself which details are most important for understanding what the author has to say. The title is important because it often tells you what the selection is about. Headings, **bold** print, *italicized* words or those in CAPITAL letters are also often important. Many paragraphs will have **topic sentences** stating the main idea of that paragraph. These sentences often identify what is most important in the passage.

CREATE MENTAL IMAGES

Much of what we know about the world comes through our five senses. When you read, try to imagine the things you are reading about. Pretend there is a miniature DVD player running inside your head. Create mental images using some or all of your five senses. Imagine what it would be like to *see*, *smell*, *hear*, *taste*, or *touch* what a character in the reading is experiencing.

MAKE PREDICTIONS

A prediction is an opinion of what will happen in the future. Good readers often make predictions as they read about what will happen next in the text. For example, if a character faces a problem, you might start thinking about some of the ways that problem could be solved. Then, as you continue reading, see if the character solves the problem using one of the ways you thought of.

SUMMARIZE

When you read, you should sometimes pause to think about what you have just read. Good readers silently summarize what is important in their own words. To summarize a text, repeat its ideas and details in a shorter form. After you complete your summary, check any important details you are not sure about before you continue. Use this strategy if you feel your mind is wandering from the reading: it will help you to stay alert and focused on what you are reading.

SOLVE PROBLEMS

If you have trouble understanding something, don't just continue reading. Take steps to figure it out. For example, good readers may re-read a difficult section several times, or check details earlier in the passage to make sure they understand it. Look back to find out who a character in the story is if you have forgotten. Try to figure out the meaning of a difficult word by looking at surrounding words and sentences, or look up the word in a dictionary.

AFTER READING

After you finish reading a selection, think about what you have just read. Think again about what was **most important** in the reading. Mentally **summarize** what the reading was about. Think about what you learned from the reading, and consider if this has changed your way of thinking about that topic. Ask yourself the following:

★ What was the message or main idea of the reading?

★ Have you learned anything *new*?

★ What were some "memorable" words and phrases?

The chart below summarizes some of the strategies used by good readers. How many of these strategies do you use when you read?

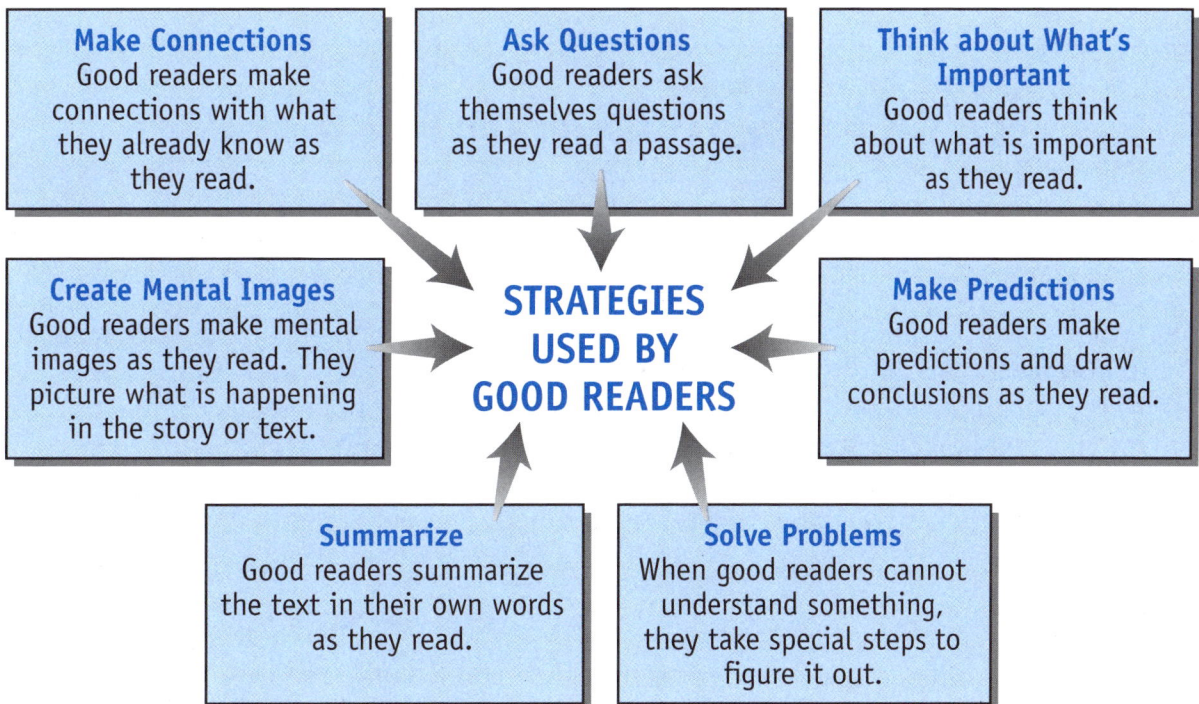

Make Connections Good readers make connections with what they already know as they read.	**Ask Questions** Good readers ask themselves questions as they read a passage.	**Think about What's Important** Good readers think about what is important as they read.
Create Mental Images Good readers make mental images as they read. They picture what is happening in the story or text.	**STRATEGIES USED BY GOOD READERS**	**Make Predictions** Good readers make predictions and draw conclusions as they read.
Summarize Good readers summarize the text in their own words as they read.	**Solve Problems** When good readers cannot understand something, they take special steps to figure it out.	

PRACTICE MODEL

Let's see how a good reader actually applies these methods. On the next page is the beginning of a sample reading selection written by a famous basketball player, Shaquille O'Neal. This model shows what a good reader thinks about *before*, *during*, and *after* reading.

Before Reading

Before reading, a good reader asks:

★ **Why am I reading this?**
I am reading this selection because I have seen Shaquille O'Neal play basketball on television, and I think it would be interesting to learn more about him.

★ **What type of text is this?**
This looks like an informational text in which the writer describes his own life.

★ **What do I already know about this subject?**
I know from watching television and reading newspapers that Shaquille O'Neal is one of the top athletes in the game of basketball.

During Reading

Chicken Soup for the **Kid's** Soul

Edited by J. Canfield   ©1998

A GOOD REASON TO LOOK UP

by Shaquille O'Neal

When I was in junior high school, what my friends thought of me was real important to me. During those years I grew much taller than most of my peers. Being so tall made me feel uncomfortable. In order to keep the focus off me and my unusual height, I went along with the crowd who would play practical jokes on other kids at school. Being one of the class clowns gave me a way to make sure that the jokes were always directed at others, and not at me.

Here are some things a good reader might think about while reading this passage:

Create Mental Images

I can just imagine how the future basketball star looked as a junior high student — much taller than most of the other kids.

What other mental images come to mind?

Ask Yourself Questions

✶ What is a "class clown"?

✶ Why did being tall make Shaq so uncomfortable?

What other questions might you ask?

Make Connections

I know some people in my school who play mean tricks on others. This article might help me to understand why they act in this way.

What other connections can you possibly make?

I would pull all kinds of pranks that were hurtful, and sometimes even harmful to others. Once before gym class, my friends and I put Icy Hot in the gym shorts of one of the kids on the basketball team. Not only was he terribly embarrassed, but he also had to go to the school nurse's office. I thought it was going to be funny, but it ended up that no one thought it was — least of all my father.

My parents didn't think that my behavior was funny at all. They reminded me about the Golden Rule: to treat others as I would like to be treated. Many times, I was disciplined for the hurtful way that I was treating others. What I was doing was hurting other kids, and in turn hurting my reputation as someone to be looked up to. My friends were looking up to me because I was tall, but what did they see?

My parents wanted me to be a leader who was a good example to others — to be a decent human being. They taught me to set my own goals, and to do my best at everything that I set out to do. During the lectures I got from my father, he told me over and over again to be the leader that I was meant to be — to be a big man in my heart and actions, as well as in my body. I had to question myself whether or not it was important to be the kind of leader and person my father believed I was inside. I knew in my heart that he was right. So I tried my best to follow my father's advice.

ASK QUESTIONS

* What is an "Icy Hot"?
* Why did Shaq think such a mean trick would be funny?
* Why do they call this the "Golden Rule"?

What other questions would you ask?

_____

_____

_____

_____

_____

THINK ABOUT WHAT IS IMPORTANT

* Did the fact that Shaq was uncomfortable with his height excuse his jokes?
* Do you try to live by the Golden Rule? Why or why not?

What else in these paragraphs would you consider to be important?

_____

_____

_____

_____

_____

Once I focused on being the best that I could be at basketball and became a leader in the game, I took my responsibility to set a good example more seriously.

I sometimes have to stop and think before I act, and I make mistakes occasionally — everyone is human. But I continue to look for opportunities where I can make a difference, and to set a good example because of my father's advice. I now pass it on to you.

"Be a leader, Shaq, not a follower. Since people already have to look up to you, give them a *good* reason to do so."

MAKE CONNECTIONS

✳ Do you try to set a good example for others in your own life? Why or why not?

_____

_____

_____

_____

SUMMARIZE

✳ Using only one or two sentences, summarize what this article was about:

_____

_____

Going Beyond the Reading

After reading a selection, a good reader thinks about what he or she has learned. Here, the reader learned some interesting facts about the early life of basketball star Shaquille O'Neal.

After reading this essay, the reader might:

★ tell a friend about Shaquille O'Neal's experiences in Junior High School;

★ add some new words — like *peers* — to a list of vocabulary words;

★ search the Internet for more information about Shaquille O'Neal's career;

★ go to the library to take out books about Shaquille O'Neal or other basketball players;

★ adopt Shaq's advice by trying to be more of a leader than a follower — a big person both in heart and actions.

CHAPTER 2

READING LITERARY TEXTS

In the eighth grade, you will mainly read two types of texts, or **genres** — literary and informational. A **literary** or **fictional** text is not written to tell you a set of facts, but to entertain and delight you. Usually, it does not tell about real events, but about make-believe events invented by the author. There are many types of literary texts, including stories, legends, poems, novels, and plays.

STORIES

Good stories can help us imagine what it would be like to live in faraway places or to enjoy exciting adventures. They teach us about other people's experiences and lives. Stories put us in touch with a wide range of emotions. They can make us laugh or cry, or make our hearts pound with excitement.

THE ELEMENTS OF A STORY

Just as every good recipe has a number of essential ingredients, every good story is made up of different elements that the author must bring together. These elements are known as:

setting   character   plot   theme

Let's look at a reading passage to illustrate the elements of a story. The story on the next page is an excerpt, or small part, from the novel *The Joy Luck Club* by Amy Tan. In this story, Jing-Mei, the daughter of a Chinese immigrant, recalls what happened after her failed attempt to play the piano at a local talent show.

JING-MEI AND HER PIANO

After the show, the Hsus, the Jongs, and the St. Clairs from the Joy Luck Club came up to my mother and father.

"Lots of talented kids," Auntie Lindo said vaguely, smiling broadly.

"That was somethin' else," said my father, and I wondered if he was referring to me in a humorous way, or whether he even remembered what I had done.

Waverly looked at me and shrugged her shoulders. "You aren't a genius like me," she said matter-of-factly. And if I hadn't felt so bad, I would have pulled her braids and punched her stomach.

But my mother's expression was what devastated me: a quiet, blank look that said she had lost everything. I felt the same way, and it seemed as if everybody were now coming up, like gawkers at the scene of an accident, to see what parts were actually missing. When we got on the bus to go home, my father was humming the busy-bee tune and my mother was silent. I kept thinking she wanted to wait until we got home before shouting at me. But when my father unlocked the door to our apartment, my mother walked and then went to the back, into the bedroom. No accusations. No blame. And in a way, I felt disappointed. I had been waiting for her to start shouting, so I could shout back and cry and blame her for all my misery.

I assumed my talent-show fiasco meant I never had to play the piano again. But two days later, after school, my mother came out of the kitchen and saw me watching TV.

"Four o'clock," she reminded me as if it were any other day. I was stunned, as though she were asking me to go through the talent-show torture again. I wedged myself more tightly in front of the TV.

"Turn off TV," she called from the kitchen five minutes later.

CONTINUED ➤

I didn't budge. And then I decided. I didn't have to do what my mother said anymore. I wasn't her slave. This wasn't China. I listened to her before and look what happened. She was the stupid one.

She came out from the kitchen and stood in the arched entryway of the living room. "Four o'clock," she said once again, louder.

"I'm not going to play anymore," I said nonchalantly. "Why should I? I'm not a genius."

She walked over and stood in front of the TV. I saw her chest was heaving up and down in an angry way.

"No!" I said, and I now felt stronger, as if my true self had finally emerged. So this was what was in me all along.

"No! I won't!" I screamed.

She yanked me by the arm, pulled me off the floor, snapped off the TV. She was frighteningly strong, half pulling, half carrying me toward the piano as I kicked the throw rugs under my feet. She lifted me up and onto the bench. I was sobbing by now, looking at her bitterly. Her chest was heaving even more and her mouth was open, smiling as if she were pleased I was crying.

"You want me to be someone I'm not!" I sobbed, "I'll never be the kind of daughter you want me to be!"

"Only two kinds of daughters," she shouted in Chinese. "Those who are obedient and those who follow their own mind! Only one kind of daughter can live in this house. Obedient daughter!"

"Then I wish I wasn't your daughter. I wish you weren't my mother," I shouted. As I said these things I got scared. It felt like worms and toads and slimy things crawling out of my chest, but it also felt good, as if this awful side of me had surfaced, at last.

"Too late change this," said my mother shrilly.

And I could sense her anger rising to its breaking point. I wanted to see it spill over. And that's when I remembered the babies she had lost in China, the ones we never talked about. "Then I wish I'd never been born!" I shouted. I wish I were dead! Like them."

CONTINUED ➤

It was as if I had said the magic word. Alakazam! — and her face went blank, her mouth closed, her arms went slack, and she backed out of the room, stunned, as if she were blowing away like a small brown leaf, thin, brittle, lifeless.

It was not the only disappointment my mother felt in me. In the years that followed, I failed her many times, each time asserting my own will, my right to fall short of expectations. I didn't get straight A's. I didn't become class president. I didn't get into Stanford. I dropped out of college.

For unlike my mother, I did not believe I could be anything I wanted to be. I could only be me.

And for all those years, we never talked about the disaster at the recital or my terrible accusations afterward at the piano bench. All that remained unchecked, like a betrayal that was now unspeakable. So I never found a way to ask her why she had hoped for something so large that failure was inevitable.

And even worse, I never asked her what frightened me the most: why had she given up hope?

After our struggle at the piano, she never mentioned my playing again. The lessons stopped. The piano lid was closed, shutting out the dust, my misery, and her dreams.

So she surprised me. A few years ago, she offered to give me the piano, for my thirtieth birthday. I had not played in all those years. I saw the piano as a sign of forgiveness, a tremendous burden removed.

"Are you sure?" I asked shyly. "I mean, won't you and Dad miss it?"

"No, this your piano," she said firmly. "Always your piano. You only one can play."

"Well, I probably can't play anymore," I said. "It's been years."

"You pick up fast," said my mother, as if she knew this was certain. "You have natural talent. You could been genius if you want to."

"No, I couldn't," I answered.

"You just not trying," said mother. And she was neither angry nor sad. She said it as if to announce a fact that couldn't be disproved. "Take it," she said.

But I didn't at first. It was enough that she had offered it to me. And after that, every time I saw it in my parents' living room, standing in front of the bay windows, it made me feel proud, as if it were a shiny trophy I had won back.

Let's see how well you applied the strategies of good readers:

BEING AN ACTIVE READER

1. What was the story about? _____
_____
_____

2. What pictures came to mind as you read the story? _____
_____

3. What questions did you have as you read the story? _____
_____
_____

4. Were there any words or ideas from the story that were difficult to understand? How did you figure them out? _____
_____
_____

Now let's take a closer look at each of the different story elements of "Jing-Mei and Her Piano" — *setting*, *characters*, *plot* and *theme*.

THE SETTING

The setting is **when** and **where** the story takes place. Often, the writer provides clues to indicate the story's time and place. For example, the language of the characters, their dress, or a description of where they are helps the reader to know the time period and place of the story.

A setting can be in the past, present, or future, or in an imaginary world where time seems hardly to exist. A story may also have more than one setting. For example, it could start in one place and end in another. Sometimes, the setting does not affect events in the story. At other times, it influences what happens.

CHECKING YOUR UNDERSTANDING

Briefly describe the **setting** of "Jing-Mei and Her Piano."

Where

Setting

When

Was the setting very important to the story? Explain. _____

_____

THE CHARACTERS

The characters of a story are **who** the story is about. Characters may be make-believe people or they may be real people in a make-believe situation. Most stories have only one or two main characters. The action in the story usually revolves around them. In "Jing-Mei and Her Piano," Jing-Mei and her mother are the main characters. Jing-Mei's mother has dreams for her daughter, but has to come to terms with Jing-Mei's growing independence.

Many stories are told from the point of view of an all-knowing narrator. Others are written from the view of one of the story characters. When a character narrates the story, it reveals something about that character. For example, would "Jing-Mei and Her Piano" be different if the mother were the narrator instead of Jing-Mei?

When reading a story, think about how the author describes the characters:

★ **How do they act?**

★ **What do the characters say?**

★ **What are they thinking and feeling?**

★ **How do the characters change as the story unfolds?**

CHECKING YOUR UNDERSTANDING

Select one character in "Jing-Mei and Her Piano" and describe that character:

CHARACTER SELECTED:
_____

THE STORY PLOT

The story plot refers to **what** takes place as the story unfolds. In most stories, the main characters face some obstacles or one character has a **conflict** with another. The plot is made up of a series of events in which the characters try to deal with these problems and conflicts. Here, Jing-Mei has a conflict with her mother.

An author usually tries to maintain the reader's interest in the story by creating some kind of suspense. As the plot unfolds, new twists arise making the main problem worse. The story ends when the main characters solve their problems or learn to accept them.

To keep track of the plot, it is often useful to make a sequence map. The sequence map below has been started for you. Complete the remaining three boxes:

Jing-Mei gives a disastrous performance at the local talent show. → Jing-Mei refuses her mother's order to practice playing the piano. →

THE STORY THEME OR LESSON

Stories often interest us because they give us a message or teach us a lesson we can apply in our own lives. This message or lesson is called the *theme* of the story. A story may have one or more themes. The theme is what makes the story important.

In "Jing-Mei and Her Piano," one lesson we learn is that as we grow up, we may develop goals for ourselves that differ from our parents' wishes.

CHECKING YOUR UNDERSTANDING

Briefly describe another **theme** of *Jing-Mei and Her Piano*. _____

_____

_____

_____

_____

POEMS

In addition to reading stories, you should know how to read and interpret poems.

WHAT IS POETRY?

All writers think about the effect their writing will have on their readers, but for poets this is even more important than for other writers. Poets explore and celebrate the qualities of language, just as artists express themselves with paint and color. They try to achieve a special harmony between what they want to say and the language they use to say it.

Like a story, many poems have a setting, characters, a plot, and a theme. Not all poems, however, tell stories. Some poems simply describe something — such as a beautiful flower, the arrival of spring, or feelings of love. Often, poets try to express their innermost feelings about the thing they are describing.

To better understand what poetry is, look at the sample poem below:

WHISPERS

Stanza 1 →
Whispers
    Tickle through your ear
        Telling you things you like to hear.

Stanza 2 →
Whispers
    Are as soft as skin
        Letting little words curl in.

Stanza 3 →
Whispers
    Come so they can blow
        Secrets others never know.

— *Myra Cohn Livingston*

As you can see, poetry is organized by lines. When reading a poem, the reader usually pauses at the end of each line. Several lines of poetry are organized into something similar to paragraphs, known as **stanzas.** The poem *Whispers* has three stanzas.

THE CHARACTERISTICS OF POETRY

Although there are several types of poetry, most poems share certain common characteristics.

RHYTHM

Poems usually have a strong rhythm. The sounds of the words have a certain beat. This rhythm is based on the pattern of syllables found on each line. Some syllables are stressed or emphasized when we say the words. When you read a poem, the stressed syllables are usually arranged so that you can hear a strong beat. It is almost as if you are reading the poem to the beat of a drum. This gives poetry a musical quality.

Poets use rhythm not only to make pleasing sounds, but also for emphasis. In the poem *Whispers,* the rhythm of the poem may actually remind us of a whisper. If you read the poem aloud, you would probably read the word "whispers" at the start of each stanza more slowly than the other lines. This creates an alternating rhythm that places greater emphasis on the word "whispers."

RHYME AND OTHER SOUND PATTERNS

Many poems are written in rhyme. This means that a word or line ends in the same sound as another word or line. For example, in the last stanza of the poem *Whispers,* the last words on the final two lines — "blow" and "know" — rhyme.

Poets use several other sound patterns besides rhyme to give poetry a musical quality. For example, they may use a series of words that begin with the same sound, like "soft as skin." Repetition of the same first sound is known as **alliteration**.

Poets may also pick words that help us to imagine or visualize what they mean. The word "whisper" itself reminds you of the kind of quiet sound that whispering makes. The word "soft" sounds gentle and soft, while in order to say "blow" we have to pucker up our cheeks and blow through our mouth. The poet has thus selected words that help us imagine what a whisper is. These words were specifically chosen by the poet. The use of words that sound like what they mean is known as **onomatopoeia**.

IMAGERY

Imagery refers to word pictures created by poets to express their feelings and ideas. Poets make greater use of images than most other writers. These vivid images help us share the poet's thoughts and feelings. For example, the author of *Whispers* wanted to express the idea that whispers are quiet and soft. To do this, she suggests a comparison between *whispers* and *soft skin.*

★ Making a comparison using "like" or "as" is known as a **simile**:
  - "I am as hungry as an ox."
  - "Whispers are as soft as skin."

★ Making a comparison by simply stating that one thing **is** another is known as a **metaphor**:
  - "An Englishman's home is his castle."
  - "Our scientists today stand on the shoulders of giants."

In *Whispers,* the poet uses imagery to appeal to all our senses. In the first stanza, she wants us to *feel* the tickle of the whisper; in the second stanza, she wants us to *hear* its softness. We not only feel the tickle and hear the softness of the whisper, we also sense the close relationship between the people whispering. When someone whispers to us, that person tells us something that is just for us. From this privilege, we take a special delight, and are told things we "like to hear." The author gives us, not only the sensation of a whisper, but also the emotions behind it. The poet has achieved all of this in only *33* words!

ANALYZING POETRY

The first question you should ask yourself when reading a poem is whether the poem tells a story or describes something. If the poet is telling a story, then you should keep track of the story elements, just like any other story. For other poems, you should be able to identify what the poem is describing and the poet's feelings about it.

Let's put what we have just learned about analyzing a poem to use. Analyze *Whispers* by completing the following:

ANALYZING A POEM

1. What is the poem mostly about? _____

_____

_____

2. What are the poet's feelings about this topic? _____

_____

_____

3. What imagery does the poet use? _____

_____

_____

4. Does the poet use: ☐ alliteration   ☐ simile

   (*check all that apply*)   ☐ onomatopoeia   ☐ metaphor

CHAPTER 3

READING INFORMATIONAL TEXTS

Another type of reading selection you should be able to recognize is an **informational text**, also known as *nonfiction*.

TYPES OF INFORMATIONAL TEXTS

Informational texts are about real people, places, events, and things. People read nonfiction to learn about real-life things. Such readings come in a wide variety of forms:

★ **Articles**. Articles are short informational pieces that are usually read in one sitting. You can find articles in newspapers, magazines, and encyclopedias. They often tell you the basic facts about something — the *who*, *what*, *where*, *why*, and *how*.

★ **Essays**. An essay gives an author's opinions and feelings about a topic or issue. Let's look at an excerpt from an essay about New York City by a well-known comedian:

LIFE INTERRUPTED

by Spalding Gray

For 34 years I lived with you and came to love you. I came to you because I loved theater and found theater everywhere I looked. I fled New England and came to Manhattan, that island off the coast of America, where human nature was king and everyone exuded character and had big attitude.

When we were kids, my Mom hung a poster over our bed. It had a picture of a bumblebee, and under the picture, the caption read:

According to all aerodynamic laws, the bumblebee cannot fly because its body weight is not in the right proportion to its wingspan. But ignoring these laws, the bee flies anyway.

That is still New York City for me.

In this essay, the author gives his feelings about New York City. *How does the essayist feel about the city*?

★ **Biographies and Autobiographies**. A biography is a text telling about some person's life and accomplishments. An autobiography is a text in which someone describes his or her own life.

All of these types of texts have something in common. They all give information about a topic. The **topic** is the subject of the reading — what it is about. The title and the first paragraph of the reading often identify its topic.

THE PARTS OF AN INFORMATIONAL READING

Just as stories have different parts, so do informational readings. There are *two* major parts to an informational reading: its *main idea* and *supporting details*.

The **main idea** states something about the topic of the reading. The **supporting details** are facts and examples that explain, describe or illustrate the main idea.

Do you know how each of these parts works? Let's look at a short informational reading. As you read this passage, remember to use the strategies of good readers — for example, *ask questions, create mental images*, and *make predictions*.

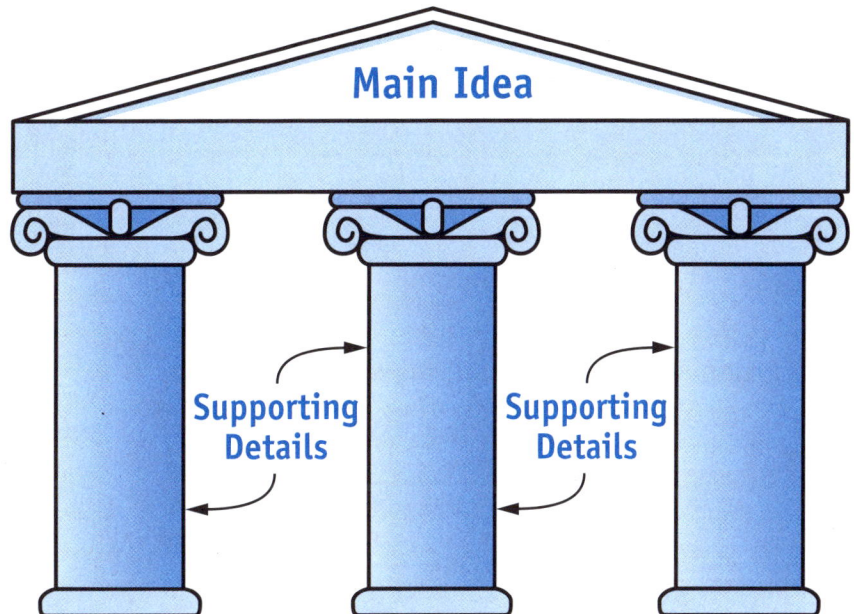

Main Idea

Supporting Details   **Supporting Details**

The passage on the next page is an article about a famous African-American singer, Marian Anderson, who lived in times when African Americans faced prejudice and discrimination. Read the article; then complete the form on page 28, applying the strategies of good readers.

MARIAN'S REVOLUTION

By Sudipta Bardhan-Quallen

By 1939, Marian Anderson had performed for presidents and kings. Despite her success, when Marian wanted to sing at Constitution Hall that year, she was banned from doing so. The owner of the hall, an organization called the Daughters of the American Revolution (or DAR), felt that Marian should not be allowed to sing there because she was African American.

That wasn't the first time Marian had been sent away because she was black. When she was 18 years old, she applied to music school. The clerk at the desk rudely sent her home because of her race. Marian was shocked at the clerk's words. "I could not conceive of a person, " Marian said, "surrounded as she was with the joy that is music without having some sense of its beauty and understanding rub off on her."

Because of segregation — the practice of keeping blacks and whites separate — the early 1900s were a difficult time for a young black woman to begin a professional singing career. But Marian was determined to sing. "It was something that just had to be done," she remembered. "I don't think I had much to say in choosing it. I think music chose me." In 1925, Marian won a voice contest in New York City, and sang with the New York Philharmonic. Still, her chances to perform in the United States were limited. To build her career, Marian traveled to Europe in 1928, where she became very successful.

Marian Anderson

By 1939, Marian was a world-class singer. But when she returned to the United States, she faced racism in many ways. Segregation was still common on trains and in hotels and restaurants. No amount of vocal talent could spare Marian from that.

Even concert halls were segregated, although usually that was limited to the audience. Because black performers often appeared on stage in segregated halls, Marian had no reason to think she would be turned away from Constitution Hall. She believed her musical skill would be the only factor the DAR would consider.

CONTINUED →

At first, the DAR told Marian that the date she requested was unavailable. Then they told her all of her alternative dates were booked. Eventually, the DAR upheld their policy that only white performers could appear in Constitution Hall.

When news of the DAR's policy got out, many people were livid. First Lady Eleanor Roosevelt (wife of President Franklin D. Roosevelt) was so outraged that she resigned from the DAR. In a letter, she wrote, "I am in complete disagreement with the attitude taken in refusing Constitution Hall to a great artist …. You had an opportunity to lead in an enlightened way and it seems to me your organization has failed."

Marian believed strongly in the civil-rights movement. She knew firsthand the pain that racism caused. She understood that the way the controversy with the DAR was resolved would be a milestone for civil rights.

Despite the public outcry, the DAR would not let Marian sing. With Mrs. Roosevelt's support, the Secretary of the Interior arranged a special concert for Marian at the Lincoln Memorial. Seventy-five thousand people attended. In many ways, Marian's concert was considered to be America's first civil-rights rally. That night, she took a stand against dis-crimination and for equality. The first words she sang were: "My country, 'tis of thee, sweet land of liberty, of thee I sing."

Anderson singing at the Lincoln Memorial April 9, 1939

Marian realized that equality in the United States would only be achieved when every person was willing to stand up for what was right. As a public figure, she felt a responsibility to set an example. After the 1939 incident, she turned down concerts for segregated audiences. "The minute a person whose word means a great deal dares to take the courageous way," she said, "many others follow."

As Marian's career progressed, America changed. She performed in many presti-gious locations, including Constitution Hall, where she sang after the DAR changed its policies. By 1954, segregation was declared unconstitutional. The Civil Rights Act was signed into law in 1964, the year Marian retired from performing. By then, many of the barriers she'd had to fight were disappearing. Marian's farewell tour began in front of an admiring crowd at Constitution Hall.

Now answer the following questions. Look back at the article as you need to.

BEING AN ACTIVE READER

1. What is the topic of this article? _____

2. What did you already know about this topic? _____
   _____

3. What information did you learn that was new? _____
   _____

4. How would you have felt if you had been Marian Anderson? _____
   _____

5. What would you have done if you had been Marian Anderson? _____
   _____

6. How important do you think Anderson's actions were to the later Civil
   Rights Movement? _____
   _____

THE MAIN IDEA OF THE READING

The general point that an author makes about the topic of a reading passage is known as the **main idea**. The *main idea* is not any particular detail. It concerns what the reading is about *as a whole*. It is the most important idea in the reading. All the details in the reading should be connected in some way to this main idea.

   For example, an author may have the idea that the person she is writing about was very kind. The author shows this by telling you about the person's good deeds. Or the author may have the idea that a place is very dangerous. The author shows this by describing the dangers experienced by visitors.

FINDING THE MAIN IDEA

When you read something for information, there are several approaches you can take to find its main idea.

LOOKING FOR A STATEMENT OF THE MAIN IDEA

Sometimes the author simply tells you the main idea in a special sentence. Often this sentence is at the beginning or the end of the reading. Therefore, examine the beginning and conclusion of the passage to see if the author directly states its main idea.

> *In "Marian's Revolution," does the author include a sentence that directly states her main idea?*

THE TOPIC APPROACH

A second way to find the main idea of a reading is to use the "topic approach." Think of this approach as a giant funnel — having a large opening at the top and a smaller opening at the bottom. This "funnel" will help lead you to the main idea.

★ **First**, determine the overall topic of the selection. As you know the topic is the subject of the reading. Often the title identifies the topic.

★ **Then**, carefully examine what the author says about the topic.

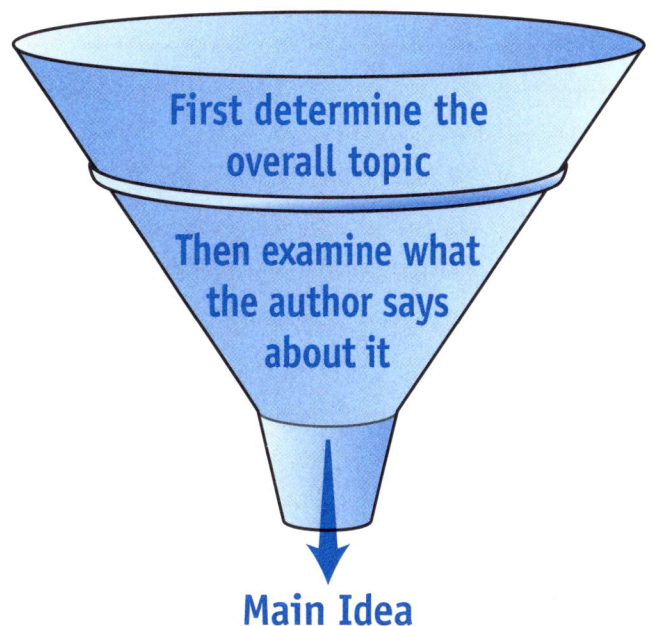

First determine the overall topic

Then examine what the author says about it

Main Idea

Look for an overall message about the topic. This message is the author's **main idea**. Other details in the reading should explain or support this main idea. The main idea is the message or general point that these details show.

> *In "Marian's Revolution," the main idea is that*
> *Anderson's reaction to her being banned from Constitution Hall*
> *contributed to the later Civil Rights Movement.*

RELATING IDEAS AND DETAILS

A third way to find the main idea is to use the "ideas and details" approach. For this approach, simply list all the major ideas and details in the selection. You can either write these out or list them in your mind. Then think about what you have listed. See if one idea covers or connects all the others. The **main idea** will be the *single most important idea* in the passage.

Sometimes the main idea is not stated directly by the author. Then you have to look at all the ideas and details you have listed and think of a main idea on your own. This should be a conclusion or general statement that all these ideas and details show.

In the article "Marian's Revolution," if you were to list all of the important ideas and details, your list might look like this:

IMPORTANT IDEAS AND DETAILS

★ Marian Anderson was a famous singer.

★ The Daughters of the American Revolution, owners of Constitution Hall, forbid Anderson to sing there in 1939 because she was African American.

★ Anderson believed she should be allowed to sing in Constitution Hall and decided to fight when she was banned.

★ First Lady Eleanor Roosevelt was outraged that the DAR banned Anderson from singing, and resigned her DAR membership.

★ Mrs. Roosevelt arranged for Anderson to sing at the Lincoln Memorial instead. Seventy-five thousand people attended the concert, considered by many to be the first "Civil Rights" rally.

★ America caught up with Anderson during the Civil Rights Movement of the 1950s.

Which of these ideas and details is general enough to cover or connect all of the other items? The answer to this question will be the **main idea** of the reading selection. Remember that the main idea connecting these other ideas and details may not be stated directly. Then you have to think of a main idea yourself that connects all the others.

THE SUPPORTING DETAILS

To help the reader understand the main idea or to prove to the reader that the main idea is true, an author supplies *examples*, *details*, and *illustrations*. It is through these details and examples that the author explains the main idea and demonstrates that it is correct.

CHECKING YOUR UNDERSTANDING

Look at the details listed in the chart on page 30. Which of these details supports the idea that Anderson's reaction to her being banned from Constitution Hall contributed to the later Civil Rights Movement?

_____

The following graphic shows the relationship between the main idea and supporting details.

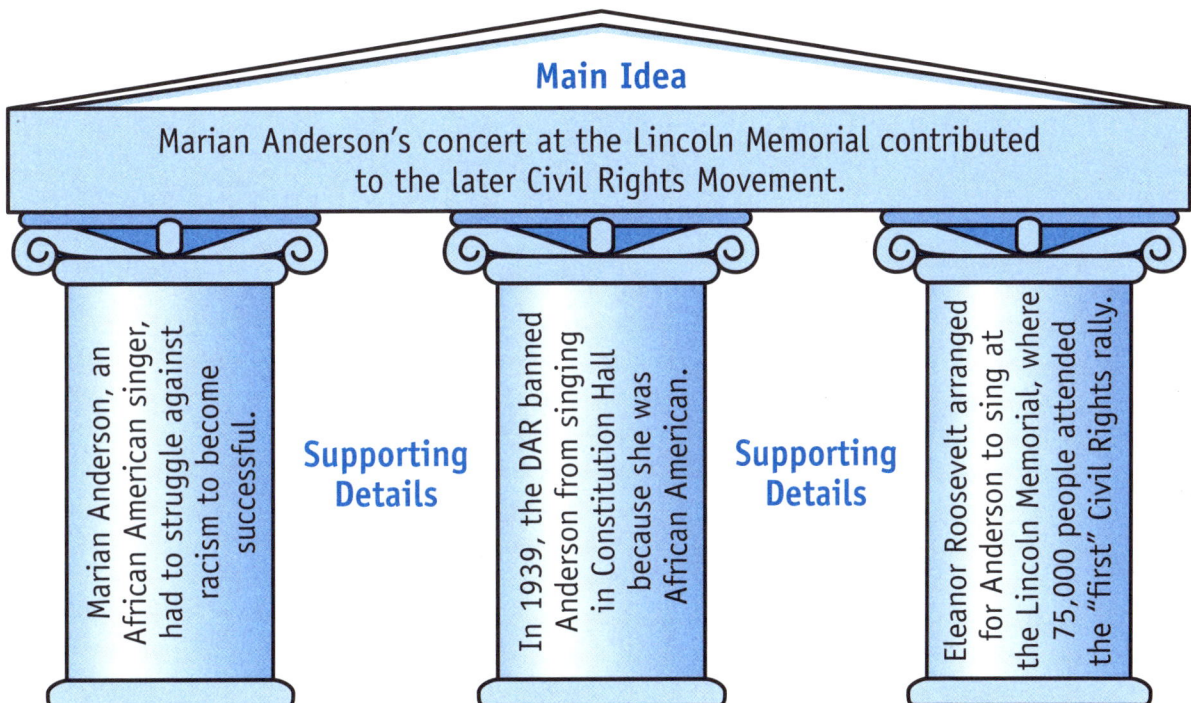

Main Idea

Marian Anderson's concert at the Lincoln Memorial contributed to the later Civil Rights Movement.

Marian Anderson, an African American singer, had to struggle against racism to become successful.

Supporting Details

In 1939, the DAR banned Anderson from singing in Constitution Hall because she was African American.

Supporting Details

Eleanor Roosevelt arranged for Anderson to sing at the Lincoln Memorial, where 75,000 people attended the "first" Civil Rights rally.

SUMMARY

In Chapters 2 and 3, you learned about two different types of readings.

IN A STORY

In a story, you can expect to find a <u>setting</u>, <u>characters</u>, <u>plot</u>, and <u>theme</u>.

IN AN INFORMATIONAL READING

In an informational reading, you can expect to find a <u>topic</u>, a <u>main idea</u> about that topic, and <u>supporting details</u>. Supporting details may include descriptions, facts, and examples.

SESSION 1: READING

Session 1 of the New York's Grade 8 English Language Arts Test consists of several reading passages. Each passage is followed by a series of multiple-choice questions. Each question has four possible choices. Your task is to select the best of the four choices to answer the question.

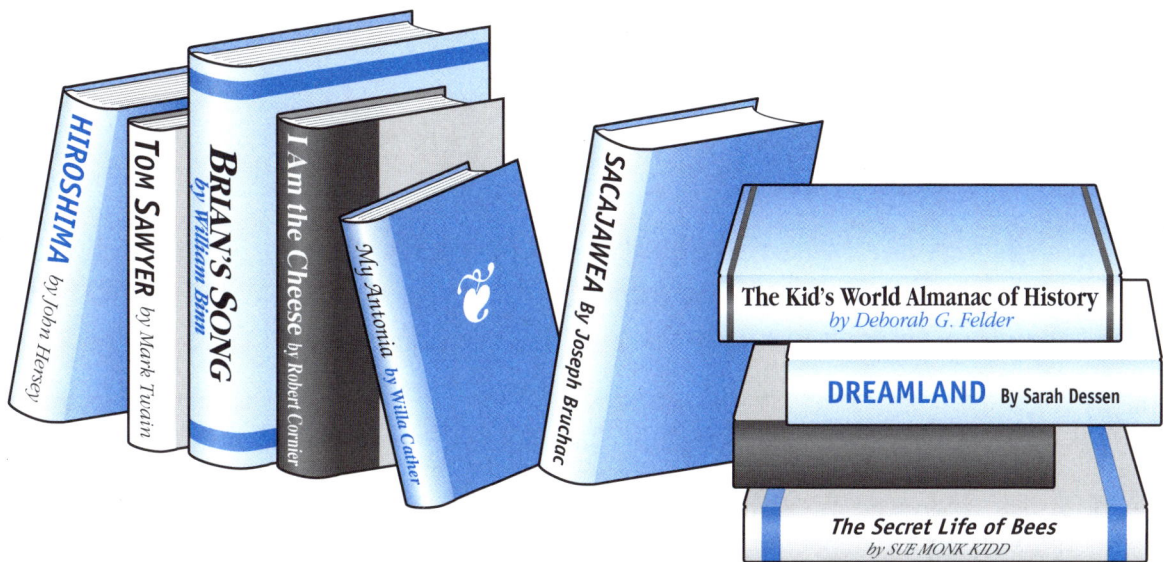

The multiple-choice questions on Session 1 of the test can be grouped into three main types. These multiple-choice questions test your ability to:

understand what the reading is about

relate specific details in the reading

evaluate and apply information from the reading

The next six chapters will examine these different types of questions in more detail. Chapter 10 has a practice test just like Session 1 of the actual English Language Arts Test that you will take later this school year.

CHAPTER 4

VOCABULARY QUESTIONS

Some of the questions on the **Grade 8 English Language Arts Test** will test your understanding of the meaning of a word or phrase used in a reading passage.

DEFINING A WORD

Many *vocabulary questions* will simply ask you what a word or phrase means. For example, read the sentences below from the article you read about Marian Anderson. Two of the more difficult words in the passage are underlined.

When news of the DAR's policy got out, many people were <u>livid</u>. First Lady Eleanor Roosevelt (wife of President Franklin D. Roosevelt) was so outraged that she resigned from the DAR. In a letter, she wrote, "I am in complete disagreement with the attitude taken in refusing Constitution Hall to a great artist…. You had an opportunity to lead in an <u>enlightened</u> way and it seems to me your organization has failed."

Now that you have finished reading this excerpt, let's see how well you can answer a *vocabulary question* about it.

1 In this paragraph, what does the word "enlightened" mean?

    A unhappy   **C** open-minded
    B ignorant   **D** prejudiced

EXPLAINING YOUR ANSWER

What is the answer? _____ Explain why you selected that answer. _____

_____

_____

_____

How would you answer this question if you were unsure about the meaning of **enlightened**? There are four techniques you can use to help you figure out the meaning of this or any other word or phrase you are unsure of:

1 SOUND OUT THE WORD

2 USE CONTEXT CLUES

3 LOOK AT PARTS OF THE WORD

4 TRY EACH ANSWER CHOICE

Not every method will always work. However, you can often combine several of these methods to figure out the meaning of most unknown words.

SOUND OUT THE WORD

To sound out a word, say the sounds of the syllables that make up the word. By sounding out a word, you may find it is a word you know or similar to a word you know.

Let's try to sound out the word "*enlightened.*" First break down the word into **syllables** (*its smaller parts*): **en-light-ened**. Then use the sounds of the letters to say each syllable. Does this sound like any word that you already know? If it does, check the answer choices to see if you can find the correct answer.

USE CONTEXT CLUES

Surrounding words and sentences often provide clues to the meaning of a difficult word or phrase. These clues are called **context clues**. They provide the background, or *context*, in which the unfamiliar word or phrase is used.

On the **Grade 8 English Language Arts Test**, there will usually be some context clues to help you answer a vocabulary question. In fact, there are several types of context clues you can use to figure out the meaning of an unfamiliar word or phrase.

DEFINING CLUES

Some neighboring phrases or sentences may actually tell you the meaning of a difficult word or phrase. These may be synonyms next to the word, phrases or clauses separated from the word by a comma, or nearby sentences. For example:

> Mr. Garcia hired the *loquacious* Mr. Brown as the new announcer for the radio station. He needed someone who was talkative and chatty.

Here, the second sentence provides a valuable clue: *loquacious* describes someone who likes to talk a lot.

CONTRAST CLUES

Some context clues will tell you what a word or phrase is **not**. For example:

> Unlike her *peripatetic* husband, Helene enjoyed staying at home reading a good book in front of her fireplace.

In this example, the use of the word "unlike" establishes a contrast in the sentence. You might be able to guess that *peripatetic* means moving around or traveling from place to place — the opposite of staying at home.

Now you try. Read the following sentence:

> Some people are vegetarians, while others are *carnivores*.

In this sentence, the phrase "*while others*" sets up a contrast. Some people eat vegetables; others eat something else. Based on this contrast, what do you think the word *carnivores* means?

COMMON-SENSE CLUES

Sometimes you need to look through an entire paragraph or several paragraphs in search of context clues. A series of details may hint at what a word or phrase means. You then have to apply your own common sense to figure this meaning out. The following are some of the most frequent common-sense clues:

Part of a Series

If the word is part of a series of things, it often names something similar to other items in the series. For example:

> Some hikers feared climbing the sharp, *precipitous* cliff.

In this example, *precipitous* is part of a series of words describing the cliff. You might guess that it has something in common with *sharp*. This could lead you to conclude that *precipitous* means very steep.

Examples in the Reading Passage

The reading passage may give examples that provide clues about the word. Knowing one or more examples can help you to figure out what the word means. Look at the following example:

> Many of these former laws have been *abrogated*. For example, people no longer have to pay poll taxes in order to vote.

What do you think *abrogated* means in this sentence? The example indicates that an *abrogated* law is one that is no longer in effect. You can conclude from these sentences that *abrogate* means to repeal, abolish or cancel something.

Cause and Effect

The passage may describe a cause or effect of the unfamiliar word. Such clues can often help you figure out what the word means. For example:

> Scientists have learned that overexposure to the sun can have very *detrimental* effects, such as skin cancer.

In this sentence, the cause of **detrimental** effects is *overexposure* to the sun. You also learn that one of the possible effects is *skin cancer*. From these clues, what do you think **detrimental** means?

Now try using a cause-and-effect clue to figure out the meaning of another word. Examine this sentence to determine the meaning of **precarious**:

> The collapse of the column left him in a **precarious** position: the platform on which he was standing could collapse at any moment.

Think about the position this person is in after the collapse of the column. Also notice that when a colon (:) is used, it often points to an effect, an example, a list, or a more detailed explanation. You can almost think of the colon as a "pointer" or "equals" sign. In this sentence, the collapse of the column is the cause and the "precarious position" is the effect. The author emphasizes this effect by explaining it in greater detail after the colon. Thus, **precarious** must be similar in meaning to something that "could collapse at any moment." What do you think **precarious** means?

Describing a Situation

The unfamiliar word or phrase may identify a situation described in the reading passage. In this case, look at the description carefully to figure out what the word or phrase means. For example:

> The woman trembled when she thought of her son's illness. She could not eat or sleep. Her hands shook and her mind wandered aimlessly. She appeared quite **distraught**.

By carefully examining the description of the woman, you can get some sense of what **distraught** might mean. The woman is distressed and upset. In fact, if you looked in the dictionary, you would find that **distraught** means "agitated with anxiety; worried."

The Tone of the Passage

The *style*, *mood*, and *tone* of the selection can also help you figure out what an unfamiliar word or phrase might mean. For example, if the author is critical of a person or action, a word describing that person or action is also likely to be critical. Just look at the paragraph below. It describes a wooden wardrobe with a broken mirror:

> It was a ***wretched*** sight. In losing the mirror, the wardrobe had lost all its life. Where the glass had once been, now there was only a rectangle of dark wood, a gloomy gap that reflected nothing and said nothing.

Let's suppose that you do not know the meaning of ***wretched***. Your first clue to its meaning should be the number of negative words and phrases used in the paragraph — *losing*, *lost*, *dark wood*, *gloomy gap*, *reflected nothing* and *said nothing*. All of these negative words should lead you to conclude that ***wretched*** refers to something negative. If you had a question asking you for the meaning of ***wretched*** in this paragraph, you should probably select the answer choice with the most negative meaning.

PARTS-OF-SPEECH CLUES

Another type of clue is the *part of speech* of the unfamiliar word. See how this unfamiliar word is used in the sentence. Does it tell about an action (*verb*), name a thing (*noun*), or describe something (*adjective*)? The correct answer should play the same role in the sentence as the unknown word. For example:

> You had an opportunity to lead in an ***enlightened*** way.....

Notice how the word ***enlightened*** is used in the sentence to describe the way that the DAR might have led others. The correct answer choice must also be an adjective (*or a phrase acting as an adjective*) describing the way that the DAR might have led others.

LOOK AT PARTS OF THE WORD

Many words are made up of different parts. For example, ***homework*** brings together the words **home** and **work**. This is known as a **compound** word.

PREFIXES

Some words have special beginnings, called **prefixes**. The word *enlightened* has the prefix *en*.

Knowing the meaning of certain common prefixes can often help you figure out the meaning of an unknown word. For example, *re*view, *re*read, *re*turn, and *re*play all begin with the prefix *re*. Usually *re* in front of a word means "to do again." Other common prefixes turn a word into its opposite — *un*, *in*, and *dis* — all mean **not**. You can see this by examining the following words: *usual* becomes <u>un*usual*</u>; *sincere* changes to <u>*in*sincere</u>; while *similar* turns to <u>*dis*similar</u>.

In the case of *enlightened*, the prefix *en* means to become or to cause something to be. Keep in mind, however, that sometimes a prefix has more than one meaning. The prefix *in* can mean *inside* as well as **not** — such as <u>*in*door</u>.

SUFFIXES

Special endings, known as **suffixes**, are also helpful in providing clues about the meaning of an unknown word. For example, *enlightened* has the suffix *ed*. Many suffixes are simply word endings for plurals or different tenses of verbs. The most common suffixes are *s*, *ed*, and *ing*. Other common suffixes change the part of speech of a word — *ly*, *er*, *ion*, *al*, *ness*, and *ment*. For example, *organize* is a *verb* that means to arrange in order. An *organization* is a noun for a group of people in an ordered relationship.

quick	quick**ly**
organize	organiza**tion**
continue	continu**al**

govern	govern**ment**
happy	happi**ness**
teach	teach**er**

ROOTS

Sometimes it helps to cover the front or back of a word to see if you can recognize any of its parts. See if you recognize the "root," or word without its beginning or ending. For example, if you cover the prefix and suffix of *enlightened*, you will see the root of the word is "*light*." To *enlighten* people is to set off a light in their heads — to make them wise, advanced or knowledgeable.

Analyzing the parts of a word, when used together with context clues, can often help you to figure out its meaning.

TRY EACH ANSWER CHOICE

The last method for answering a *vocabulary question* is to try putting each answer in place of the unfamiliar word. Think about what the author is trying to say in the sentence. Select the word or group of words that seems to make the most sense.

For example, look at the question and answer choices that appeared earlier in this chapter on page 34. Read each one in place of *enlightened* in the sentence:

> *You had an opportunity to lead in an **enlightened** way, and it seems to me your organization has failed.*

A You had an opportunity to lead in an ⟨ *unhappy* ⟩ way, and it seems to me your organization has failed.

B You had an opportunity to lead in an ⟨ *ignorant* ⟩ way, and it seems to me your organization has failed.

C You had an opportunity to lead in an ⟨ *open-minded* ⟩ way, and it seems to me your organization has failed.

D You had an opportunity to lead in a ⟨ *prejudiced* ⟩ way, and it seems to me your organization has failed.

★ **Choice A** is wrong. We know that enlightened is associated with "light" — it is a positive word and "unhappy" is not positive.

★ **Choice B** is wrong. Roosevelt believed that the DAR lost an opportunity. Being ignorant would not have been an opportunity. In fact, in this context, ignorant is almost the opposite of ***enlightened***.

★ **Choice D** is also wrong. It would not make sense to say that someone had an opportunity to act in a "prejudiced" way, or to be angry that they were not prejudiced. Usually, someone would be glad to avoid prejudiced actions.

The best answer choice is therefore **C**. It makes the most sense in this context. The DAR had an opportunity to lead, but it failed to make use of this opportunity. It makes sense that this opportunity was an "open-minded" one. We know that "enlightened" comes from the root word "light." Something "light" is generally viewed as positive. Notice that "open-minded" is the most positive of the four answer choices.

Here are some of the strategies used by good readers to answer *vocabulary questions* asking you define a word or phrase:

NOTE: *Throughout this book, you will find special "Strategies for Success" features. Just as a game of chess requires you to use various strategies to plan your moves, this book will help you to apply different strategies and techniques for answering each type of question on the **Grade 8 English Language Arts Test**. Think of each of these features as a strategy to use for attacking that kind of question on the test.*

STRATEGIES FOR SUCCESS

♛ **First**, read the question carefully to determine what it asks for.

♜ **Next**, turn to the reading selection to see how the word is used. If you need to decipher an unfamiliar word:

    ★ Say the word to yourself.

    ★ Decide what part of speech the word is.

    ★ Look for defining, contrasting, and common-sense context clues in surrounding words and sentences.

    ★ See if you can break the word apart into its *prefix*, *root*, and *suffix*.

♞ **Finally**, look over the answer choices. Substitute each answer choice in place of the word or phrase. Then choose the one that makes the most sense.

SYNONYMS AND ANTONYMS

You might also be asked to select a word or phrase which means the **same as** or the **opposite** of a word used in the passage. A *synonym* is a word with a similar meaning. An *antonym* is a word with the opposite meaning.

To answer questions about synonyms and antonyms, try the following approach:

STRATEGIES FOR SUCCESS

First, look over the question to determine if it asks for a **synonym** or an **antonym**:

★ **Synonyms.** A synonym is another word with a similar meaning. For example, here are some synonyms for the word "outraged": *enraged, angered, incensed, exasperated, offended, shocked, infuriated*.

★ **Antonyms.** To select an opposite, think of a word that deals with the same thing in the opposite direction. Here are some opposites: *hard / soft*; *day / night*; *noisy / quiet*; and *sick / well*.

Next, decide what the word or phrase in the reading passage means. Use context clues, parts of speech clues and parts of the word to help you figure it out.

Finally, examine the answer choices to select the word or phrase that is either **similar** to or the **opposite** of the word in the passage.

Now let's apply these strategies to answer the following question:

2 Read these sentences from the paragraph on page 34.

> **When news of the DAR's policy got out, many people were livid. First Lady Eleanor Roosevelt (wife of President Franklin D. Roosevelt) was so outraged that she resigned from the DAR.**

Which of the following has a meaning most similar to the word "livid"?

F lively   H furious
G comfortable   J content

EXPLAINING YOUR ANSWER

What is the answer? _____ Explain why you selected that answer. _____

_____

_____

Which answer choice makes the most sense? The first sentence tells us that when the DAR's decision came out, many people were *livid*. The second sentence provides an important context clue. We learn that Eleanor Roosevelt was so outraged by the decision that she resigned from the DAR. Like many other people, she became *livid* when she heard the news. Thus, *livid* is close in meaning to "outraged." From these context clues, you can also conclude that *livid* must be something negative. "Furious" is the only negative word among the four answer choices. It means angry or outraged. Therefore, "furious" is the word closest in meaning to "livid."

3   Read this sentence from the paragraph on page 34.

> **She performed in many prestigious locations, including Constitution Hall, where she sang after the DAR changed its policies.**

Which of the following words means the opposite of "prestigious" in this sentence?

A   distinguished
B   unimportant
C   respected
D   prominent

WORDS WITH MULTIPLE MEANINGS

Many words in the English language have more than one meaning. The same word may even be used for different parts of speech — such as a noun, adjective, or verb. Some questions on the **Grade 8 English Language Arts Test** may examine your understanding of how a word with multiple meanings is used in a passage. You could be asked to identify which definition of the word is being used. To answer this kind of question, look back at the reading for context clues that tell how the word is used.

PRACTICE EXERCISE

Read the following paragraph. Then answer the questions that follow.

The 1840s in Ireland are remembered as one of the country's darkest times. Ireland had suffered religious, cultural, and political persecution for centuries. But the Great Potato Famine of 1845 to 1849, which destroyed a staple crop of the Irish people, added one more atrocity that made life so miserable that millions fled the country, many coming to America. These Catholic tenant farmers became the Irish-American middle class, rising to prominence in labor, politics, and law enforcement.

Irish immigrants fleeing to America

4 Read this sentence from the article.

> **But the Great Potato Famine of 1845 to 1849, which destroyed a staple crop of the Irish people, added one more atrocity that made life so miserable that millions fled the country, many coming to America.**

In this sentence, the word "staple" means

F   delicious   H   basic
G   unpopular   J   unhealthy

5 Which word has a meaning opposite to that of "atrocity" in the sentence above?

A   outrage   C   kindness
B   misery   D   horror

6 Read this sentence from the article.

> **These Catholic tenant farmers became the Irish-American middle class, rising to prominence in labor, politics, and law enforcement.**

In this sentence, a "tenant farmer" is someone who

F   follows the Catholic religion   H   rents land to farm
G   comes from Ireland   J   belongs to the middle class

CHAPTER 5

FINDING THE MAIN IDEA

When you start to read a text, you usually have very little idea of what it will say. But as you read further, you begin to develop a general sense of what the text is about. You try to grasp its main idea. As you continue reading, your understanding of this main idea may change. Your mind continuously jumps back and forth between this main idea and specific details in the reading.

Some questions on the **Grade 8 English Language Arts Test** will test how well you can identify the **main idea** of a text. These questions may be stated in a variety of ways:

What is this story mainly about?	**What is the main idea of the article?**	**What is another title for the poem?**

How you answer *main idea questions* will largely depend on whether the reading selection is a ***story***, ***poem*** or an ***informational reading***. Let's examine each of these types to see how you should go about finding its **main idea**.

STORIES

When you see a *main idea* or *mostly-about question* about a story, look carefully at the answer choices. The best answer will describe what happens in the ***entire story*** rather than just a part of it.

Often each answer choice will provide a very short summary telling what is important to the story. This usually includes the problem facing the main character(s) in the story and how it is resolved. However, the answer choices may not be this specific. They may just identify the main character and indicate what happens to him or her. For this reason, it is important that you compare the answer choices carefully. A good way to approach such a question is to pretend that a friend has asked you about the story. You have only **one sentence** to tell your friend about it. What information would you provide?

46

Read the story below about two brothers. Then practice answering a question asking what the story is mostly about.

THE HERO OF INDIAN CLIFF

By C. H. Claudy

High in the mountains, two brothers climbed a steep cliff. The older brother carried a knapsack of food, a water canteen, and a long coil of rope. Sometimes, when the trail grew steep, he would tie the rope around a tree and throw the other end to his brother to make it easier for him to follow.

"Get a good grip on the rope, Nando," he called, "and watch where you put your feet."

For a year Nando had been waiting for this hike. Today he was nine years old. For his birthday, his brother Manuel was showing him the way to a secret lookout — Indian Cliff! Manuel was twelve, and had been coming to Indian Cliff for two years. Today Manuel went slowly to help Nando, since he sometimes climbed too fast and could hardly keep up.

Finally they reached a place where the path grew level. Below, Nando could see the valley where he lived. The highway running up the valley looked like a thin black ribbon. His school seemed no bigger than a matchbox. Across the fields he could see his town.

"This is it — my secret lookout," Manuel said, "I'll show you why I call it Indian Cliff." He reached into the hollow of a tree. When he pulled his hand out, it held three small sharp arrowheads. "I found them lying on the trail," Manuel said proudly, "I think Indians used to camp here."

The boys found two rocks for seats close to the edge of the cliff. Manuel took sandwiches from his knapsack. After they ate, Manuel stood to stretch his legs.

Then it happened without warning! The rock Manuel was standing on suddenly shifted. It slid down the slope toward the cliff, carrying Manuel with it!

CONTINUED ➡

Manuel yelled and tried to catch hold of something. His feet struck a ledge, and he stopped — but the ledge crumbled, and he felt himself sliding again. His fingers grabbed a rock, and he came to a halt. He looked down and saw his legs dangling over the side of Indian Cliff.

"Nando!" he screamed. "The rope! Tie it around a tree, and lower it down to me." Nando scrambled along the top of the cliff. A little bit of earth, loosened from above, struck him on the shoulders. What if a large rock should come down before Nando could get the rope?

"But it won't," Manuel thought to himself. "Nando will send the rope down — and then I'll get out of this mess." Manuel then had a horrible thought: "What if the rope isn't long enough to reach me?"

With each passing second, it grew harder to hold on. Far above, Nando was lowering a rope! Moving slowly, catching on bits of rock and then dropping again, the end of the rope came gradually nearer. And then it stopped — just a few inches above Manuel's hands! "It's no good!" Manuel yelled. "I can't reach it!"

A second later the rope rose a short way back up the cliff. It hung there, its end waving in the air. Then it started down again — this time it reached Manuel with two feet to spare. Manuel began to pull himself up. He pulled with his arms, and pushed with his legs by sticking his feet into cracks in the cliff. Halfway up the rope seemed to give a little, and he heard a cry from Nando somewhere above.

Manuel was only five feet from the top — now three feet — only one foot — now safety! With a shout of joy he pulled himself onto the top of the cliff. At once he saw his little brother lying on his stomach, his arms locked tightly around the tree. The rope was knotted around one of his ankles. There had not been enough rope to reach Manuel, so Nando had made it longer with his own body.

Manuel fell on the ground beside Nando, and burst into sobs of relief. Nando sat up, his face shining with joy. Nando's ankle was bruised and raw from the rope.

CONTINUED ➤

Manuel helped him stand and told him to lean on his arm. Together they started back down the trail toward home.

"I was scared, Manuel, real scared." Nando said.

"I know," Manuel answered. "I was scared too."

They walked slowly, helping each other along. "One more thing," Manuel said. "I'll never come back to Indian Cliff without my little brother to look after me."

1   The story "The Hero of Indian Cliff" is mainly about how

   A   a boy takes his younger brother hiking for his birthday
   B   two boys collect Indian arrowheads in the mountains
   C   a boy saves his older brother from falling down a cliff
   D   two brothers view their hometown from an ancient lookout

EXPLAINING YOUR ANSWER

What is the answer? _____ Using story details, explain why you picked that answer. _____

_____

Did you select the right answer? Could you tell that three of the answer choices focused on specific details in the story rather than on the story as a whole? Let's take a closer look at each of these answer choices:

★   **Choice A** tells how the boys go hiking but not the main problem they face — that Manuel almost falls down the cliff.

★   **Choice B** tells how the boys collect arrowheads, but again omits the main problem they face.

★   **Choice D** tells how two brothers looked down at their hometown from the mountain, but again fails to tell about the main problem of the story, Manuel's fall and Nando's rescue.

Only **Choice C** really gets to the main point of the story. It succinctly states the problem — that one of the brothers almost falls down the cliff — and the solution — that he is saved by his younger brother. **Choice C** is the best answer because it summarizes in one sentence what is really important to the story. It identifies all a person needs to know to understand what the story is about.

Sometimes a *main idea question* about a story may ask for its theme or universal message. You should look carefully at the answer choices to see what the question is really asking for. You will have more practice with *theme questions* later in this book.

When you see a *main idea question* about a story, follow these steps:

STRATEGIES FOR SUCCESS

First, identify the main character or characters in the story.
- ★ What is the main problem they face?
- ★ How do they resolve this problem?

Next, see if you can think of a *single sentence* that summarizes what happens in the story.

Finally, look over the answer choices. Pick the choice closest to your sentence expressing the main idea of the story. Answers that just give specific details from the story, rather than what is important to the story as a whole, will usually *not* be correct.

POEMS

You may also be asked to identify the "main idea" of a poem. Remember that there are two types of poems. Some poems ***tell a story***. Others ***express the poet's feelings*** about something — an event, an object, or another person.

- ★ If the poem tells a story, you should answer a *main idea question* about it just as you would answer a *main idea question* about any other story.

- ★ If the poem expresses the poet's feelings about something, then the "main idea" should identify what the poet is writing about and how the poet feels about it.

On the next page is a poem by Emily Dickinson (1830–1886), an American poet who became famous when her poems were published after her death. Read the poem and then answer the question that follows.

MORNING

by Emily Dickinson

Will there really be a morning?
    Is there such a thing as day?
Could I see it from the mountains
    If I were as tall as they?

Has it feet like water-lilies?
    Has it feathers like a bird?
Is it brought from famous countries
    Of which I have never heard?

Oh, some scholar! Oh, some sailor!
    Oh, some wise man from the skies!
Please to tell a little pilgrim
    Where the place called morning lies.

Emily Dickinson

2   What is the main idea of the poem *Morning*?

    F   Each morning is something almost unreal.
    G   Morning seems to come to us from another place.
    H   Scholars cannot tell where morning comes from.
    J   Only mountains can see where morning comes from.

EXPLAINING YOUR ANSWER

What is the answer? _____ Using details from the poem, explain why you picked that answer. _____

_____

In this poem, Dickinson does not tell a story. Instead, she writes about the morning. She opens the poem by asking if there really will be a morning. Then she asks several questions about where morning comes from. Can the tall mountains see where the morning comes from? Do they see if the morning rests on feet like a water-lily, or rises up with feathered wings, like a bird?

Answer choices F, H, and J focus on particular details of the poem. Only choice G focuses on the poem as a whole. It states the poem's main idea — that each morning seems to come to us from another place.

Here's another poem by Emily Dickinson. Read the poem and then answer the question that follows.

THE GRASS
by Emily Dickinson

The grass so little has to do, —
    A sphere of simple green,
With only butterflies to brood,
    And bees to entertain,

And stir all day to pretty tunes
    The breezes fetch along,
And hold the sunshine in its lap
    And bow to everything;

And thread the dews all night, like pearls,
    And make itself so fine,
A duchess were too common
    For such a noticing.

And even when it dies, to pass
    In odours so divine,
As lowly spices gone to sleep,
    Or amulets of pine.

Amulet. Jewelry worn to protect against evil, injury or bad luck.

3 What is the main idea of the poem?

    A Blades of grass have little to do except to entertain bees.
    B Drops of dew form on blades of grass at night.
    C Grass goes through its own life cycle, from day and night to hay.
    D Grass is green in color and has an odor that is divine.

EXPLAINING YOUR ANSWER

What is the answer? _____ Using details from the poem, explain why you picked that answer. _____

_____

_____

INFORMATIONAL READINGS

You already know that most informational readings have a main idea and supporting details. The main idea is what the author is trying to show or explain. It is like a thread running through all the paragraphs of the text. A *main idea question* about an informational reading could ask for the main idea in one of several ways:

What is the passage mainly about?	**What is the main idea of the passage?**	**What is the best title for the passage?**

Depending on the answer choices, the question may be asking for either the **topic** of the passage or for a short statement of the author's **main idea**. Again, it is important to look at the answer choices to understand what the question is really asking for.

Remember, there are several ways to identify the **main idea** of an informational reading:

★ **Look for a Statement of the Main Idea.** First, look at the title for clues. Then see if there is a sentence near the beginning or end of the reading in which the author directly states the main idea of the passage.

★ **Relating Ideas and Details.** You can list all the important ideas or facts mentioned in the reading. Then see which idea seems to cover all the others.

★ **The Topic Approach.** Often the main idea is *not* directly stated. First, determine the **topic** (*subject*) of the reading. For example, is the text about an event, a person, or an idea? Then, see what the author has to say about it. The author's *message* about the topic is the **main idea**.

Let's see how well you can identify the main idea of an informational passage. Read the following article about Dorothea Lange, a famous photographer.

SEEING THROUGH DOROTHEA'S EYES
by Sudipta Bardhan

Every day after school Dorothea Lange walked through the streets of downtown Manhattan, heading for the library where her mother worked. She moved so quietly that no one really noticed her at all. Dorothea didn't mind going unnoticed — it gave her a chance to see the things she wanted to see.

Dorothea had a difficult childhood because she felt different from others. She had a physical disability. When she was seven, she contracted polio, which left her walking with a limp. When she was twelve, her father abandoned their family. Dorothea became a solitary child. When her mother went to work, she spent many hours alone, watching other people going about their lives.

Dorothea Lange and her camera

Over time, Dorothea developed a special gift— she saw beauty in things that others didn't even notice. As she walked the streets of New York City, she discovered a world full of images. She saw poor immigrants struggling to make lives for themselves in America. She saw the homeless walking the same streets as the wealthy. Even before she held a camera in her hands, Dorothea captured these images in her mind and heart.

One of Dorothea's journeys led her to Arnold Genthe, a portrait photographer. She didn't have much experience with photography, but in 1914 she convinced Genthe to make her his assistant. He taught her how to take portraits and work with cameras, lights, and negatives. She watched everything he did and soon became an accomplished photographer.

In 1919, Dorothea Lange traveled to San Francisco. She set up her own portrait studio and became successful photographing the rich and famous.

Ten years later, when the Great Depression began, things changed for everyone, including Lange. People all over the country lost their jobs. Businesses closed, and fewer people could afford Lange's portraits.

CONTINUED

Lange struggled to decide what to do next. Walking alone one day, she remembered the images she still had from her childhood of hard-working immigrants. Suddenly, she knew what she had to do.

Lange wandered the streets of San Francisco, just as she had done as a child in New York City. She watched people going about their lives. One day, she took a photo of people waiting in a bread line. She hung that photo in her studio and realized that it was more powerful than all of the work she had done before.

The State of California soon hired Lange to photograph the living conditions of migrant farm workers.[1] She traveled to the camps where migrants from the Midwest came looking for work. In one camp, she came across a woman and her family on the brink of starvation. "I approached the hungry and desperate mother. She said they had been living on frozen vegetables and birds the children killed."

Lange was appalled by the way these families were living. She took photographs of the woman and her children, and others in the camp. When people saw her photographs, they were shocked. In fact, the federal government rushed food to the workers in that camp, mainly because Lange had brought attention to them.

This photo of a 32-year-old mother of seven children showed the living conditions of migrant farm workers.

The pictures Lange took during the Great Depression captured people's despair and hopelessness. But they also captured their pride and honor. She saw a determination in people that even the Great Depression could not take away. Using her camera, Lange kept a record of people who would have otherwise been forgotten. When President Franklin Roosevelt began a program to help people most affected by the Depression, Dorothea's photos played an important role in bringing aid to many migrant workers.

Throughout her life, Lange believed that "a camera is an instrument that teaches people how to see." The pictures she made decades ago still teach us to see that strength and determination of the human spirit.

---

[1]**migrant workers:** people who travel from place to place to work

4   Which sentence **best** summarizes the main idea of this article?

    F   Dorothea spent much of her time watching others because she had polio as a child.

    G   Dorothea's unique experiences helped her to take photographs capturing the despair of the Great Depression.

    H   Dorothea's photograph of a woman in a migrant camp encouraged the government to give migrants special relief.

    J   Dorothea became a successful portrait photographer in San Francisco.

Let's see if we can guide you towards the right answer to this question. Think about the questions below to see if you answered this *main idea question* correctly.

POINTING THE WAY

➡ What is the **topic** of the reading? _____

➡ List some of the most important ideas and facts the author presents about this topic:

    1. _____

    2. _____

    3. _____

    4. _____

➡ Select one of the ideas above as the main idea, or write down the "main idea"

    on your own: _____

    _____

➡ Which answer choice is closest to your statement of the main idea? _____

Remember that some *main idea* or *mostly about questions* may just ask you for the **topic** of the reading. Others will ask you to identify what the author has to say about the topic. Look over the answer choices to see what kind of question it really is.

The following page highlights some of the steps used by good readers to find the main idea of an informational text:

STRATEGIES FOR SUCCESS

First, think about the **topic** or subject matter of the reading. Often the title will tell you its topic. In this article, the title — "Seeing through Dorothea's Eyes" — helps identify the topic: *Dorothea Lange*.

Next, think about the article's chief message about that topic. Sometimes the reading itself will state the main idea in a topic sentence at the beginning or end of the selection. Otherwise, try to think of a single sentence that expresses the main idea of what you read. Can you summarize what the author says about Dorothea Lange in a single sentence?

Finally, look over the answer choices. Pick the choice closest to your sentence expressing the main idea of the article. Answers that give specific details from the article are usually *not* the main idea. For example, the article tells how Dorothea became a portrait photographer in San Francisco. However, this detail is only one part of the article — it does not cover the whole article and is **not** the main idea.

Skimming is an important skill that can help you find the "big picture" — the main idea — of a reading.

— SKIMMING —

When you skim, you read quickly through a passage to get a general sense of what it is all about. You can use skimming with a story, article or any other type of text.

HERE ARE TWO COMMON WAYS TO SKIM:

★ Some people skim by first looking at the title, illustrations, captions and special headings of the reading. Then they read the first and last paragraph of the passage more carefully. This helps them to get a general sense of what the passage is all about.

★ Other good readers "speed read" through the entire passage. They force their eyes to move along the page at a much faster rate than normal. They sometimes stop at topic sentences to read them more slowly.

Whatever way of skimming you use, just remember that you are not trying to read every word when you skim. You are just "skimming" the surface to see what the passage is about. You can always read the selection more carefully a second time to grasp the details.

— READING FOR A PURPOSE —

Experts find that good readers read for a purpose. This helps them decide which information is important. When you read a passage during a test, your main purpose is to understand the text and answer questions about it. This purpose, however, is too general to guide your reading. It is impossible to memorize every detail in the reading. Therefore, what should you focus on?

In test situations, good readers find it often helps to focus on the **main idea** of the passage and how the author uses details to support it. The way this is done for each *genre* is slightly different:

IF YOU ARE READING A STORY:

★ Look for **when** and **where** it takes place.
★ Focus on the **characters** and the **problems** they face.
★ *Visualize* what happens to the characters as the story progresses.

Imagine that the story is a movie unfolding in your head as you read.

IF YOU ARE READING A POEM:

★ Decide what **kind** of poem it is.
★ Think about the **author's feelings** and how these are expressed.

Say the words of the poem silently to yourself as you read them. When you read a poem, listen to its music.

IF YOU ARE READING AN INFORMATIONAL PASSAGE:

★ Identify the author's **topic**.
★ Think about what the author has to say about the topic (the **main idea**).
★ Think about how the author supports or explains this message.

Try to have an **internal dialogue** in your mind about what the author says. Ask questions, make connections and draw conclusions. Decide if you agree with what the author has to say.

CHAPTER 6

LOOKING AT THE DETAILS

Now that you have considered the "main idea" of a reading passage, let's look more carefully at the details in the reading and how they relate. You can think of looking at the "big picture" as viewing the reading from a distance through a telescope. Now you will examine the same passage with a magnifying glass.

FINDING DETAILS

Some questions on the **Grade 8 English Language Arts Test** may simply ask you to recall a particular detail from the reading. You either have to remember this detail or find it in the text to answer the question.

Let's look at a sample question based on the article you read in the last chapter, "Seeing through Dorothea's Eyes."

> **Note:** *You may want to review the article on pages 54 to 55, since many of the questions in this chapter deal with that passage.*

1 What event left Dorothea walking with a limp?

    A a car accident   **C** a childhood illness

    B a careless medical procedure   **D** a birth defect

EXPLAINING YOUR ANSWER

What is the answer? _____ Write out the sentence from the article that provided the answer. _____

_____

To answer *detail questions*, you should know how to scan a reading.

— SCANNING —

When you **scan**, you read through a passage quickly to locate specific information. Think of scanning as a treasure hunt. You are searching through the text to find a piece of buried treasure.

Here is a technique many good readers use when they scan:

★ Scan by looking for **key words**. For example, this question asks why Dorothea walked with a limp. Look for places in the reading where the name **Dorothea** and terms like **limp** or **childhood** appear. If you were looking for a specific date in the reading, then you might just scan for numbers.

★ Force your eyes to race along the page. The idea is not to read each sentence. Instead, only stop each time you see the key words **Dorothea**, **limp** or **childhood**. If that sentence does not have the information you need, continue to scan the rest of the text.

★ Once you locate the information you are looking for, focus in and read that sentence or group of sentences more carefully.

Although similar in some ways, *scanning* is different from *skimming*. When you **skim**, you quickly read through the whole passage to get a general idea of what it is about. When you **scan**, your focus is different. When scanning, you quickly read through the passage to locate *specific* information.

To answer Question 1 on page 59, first scan the passage. Often the answer will be found directly in the text. The answer to this question is in the second paragraph — Dorothea contracted polio as a child, leaving her with a limp when she walked.

Let's continue with an additional *detail question*. Answer the question on the next page based on what you recall. Then scan the article to see if you are correct.

2   How did Dorothea become a professional photographer?

    F   She watched other people while growing up in New York City.

    G   She assisted a well-known portrait photographer.

    H   She took a course in professional photography in California.

    J   She was hired by the government during the Great Depression.

SEQUENCE QUESTIONS

Some questions may ask how details in the reading are related. For example, a question could ask about the sequence or order of events:

| What happened before or after an event in the article? | Which event occurred first? | Which is the correct order of events in the story? |

This kind of question tests how well you understand the order of events in the passage. Let's try answering a *sequence question* about the same article.

3   Which event in Dorothea Lange's life took place **last**?

    A   She studied poor immigrants on the streets of New York City.

    B   She opened her own photography studio in San Francisco.

    C   She photographed migrant workers during the Great Depression.

    D   She worked with Arnold Genthe, a portrait photographer.

POINTING THE WAY

➡ Look through the article to see when each event happened. Then make a timeline of the four events listed as answer choices.

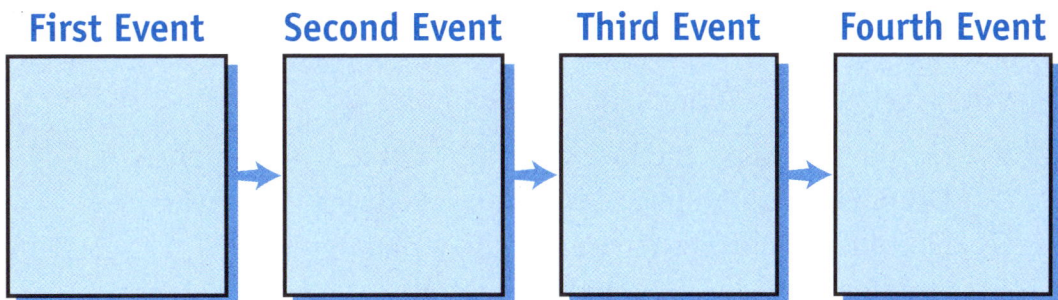

| First Event | Second Event | Third Event | Fourth Event |

➡ What is the correct answer choice? _____

To answer a question about the sequence of events, here is a strategy often used by good readers:

STRATEGIES FOR SUCCESS

First, scan the reading to find the events listed in the question.

Next, pay attention to the order of those events. Remember, most writers present events in the order in which they have taken place. The author will tell you if an event is out of sequence. For example, a character may remember something from the past (known as a *flashback*.)

★ Number the events in the margins of the passage or make a list of the order in which they appeared.

★ Make a simple diagram, such as a timeline, showing the order of events in the reading.

Finally, look over the answer choices. Pick the answer that states the correct order of events.

4 Look at the following diagram, which shows information from the article.

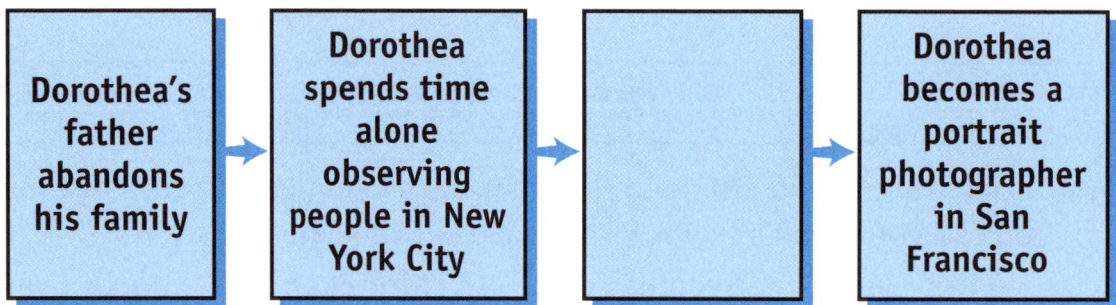

| Dorothea's father abandons his family | → | Dorothea spends time alone observing people in New York City | → | | → | Dorothea becomes a portrait photographer in San Francisco |

Which of these best completes the diagram?

F Dorothea sees people lose their jobs in the Great Depression.
G Dorothea photographs a woman on the brink of starvation.
H Dorothea is hired as an assistant to a photographer.
J Dorothea develops a limp from polio.

EXPLAINING YOUR ANSWER

Put the four events in the question in chronological order by placing a number next to each answer choice. Now, what do you think is the answer? _____

1. _____   3. _____

2. _____   4. _____

CAUSE-AND-EFFECT QUESTIONS

Some questions may test your understanding of cause-and-effect.

★ The **cause** of something is what made it happen. For example, if you turn on a light switch, you cause the light to go on. Questions asking for a cause often begin with the word **why**.

★ The **effect** of something is what happens as a result. The effect of your turning on the light switch is that the light goes on.

CAUSE Someone turned on the switch.

EFFECT The light went on.

Often, key words in the reading will help you answer the question. These key words include: **why**, **because**, **as a result**, and **in order to**. Quite often something happens because of the actions of one or more individuals. Think about why these people acted as they did. The **reason why** someone did something often explains **why** it occurred. Always think about the **motives** of the people involved when answering a question about *why* an event took place.

Now let's practice answering some *cause-and-effect questions.*

5   According to the article, why did the federal government rush food supplies to the migrant workers' camp that Dorothea photographed?

   A   A newspaper campaign called for their relief.
   B   Federal officials were moved by Dorothea's photograph.
   C   The migrants went on hunger strikes for better conditions.
   D   The people in the photograph were threatening to riot.

EXPLAINING YOUR ANSWER

What is the answer? _____ Write the sentence in the article that supports your answer choice. _____

_____

Did you discover any special strategies for answering *cause-and-effect questions*? Here is the strategy often used by good readers when answering such questions.

STRATEGIES FOR SUCCESS

First, look over the question carefully.

Next, find the events the question is asking about:
  ★ Use key words and other clues to find the **cause** of something. Think how a person's motives and actions might have *caused* the event. Questions asking for a *cause* will usually ask why something happened, the reasons for it, or for an explanation of why it occurred.
  ★ For **effects**, think about what happened because of that event. Questions asking for an *effect* will usually ask for a result of something, a consequence or an outcome of it. To explain why an event is important, also think about its *effects*.

Finally, look over the answer choices. Pick the choice that states the correct *cause* or *effect* of the event in the question.

Let's practice this strategy by answering two more questions about the same reading passage. If you need to, you may look back at the text to find your answers.

6   Why did Dorothea's business suffer when the Great Depression struck?

  F   Dorothea was too upset by the poverty she witnessed.
  G   Fewer people could afford to have their photographs taken.
  H   The federal government terminated her work contract.
  J   A childhood disability made it difficult for her to work.

7   According to the article, what was an important effect of Dorothea Lange's photography?

    A   It helped lead to a recovery from the Great Depression.

    B   It persuaded famous people to help care for poor migrant workers.

    C   It convinced the federal government to close down public bread lines.

    D   It left an important record of the suffering of the Great Depression.

COMPARE-AND-CONTRAST QUESTIONS

Compare-and-contrast questions ask you to compare two or more characters, persons, or things. Usually, the question will ask you how the items are similar or different. A *compare-and-contrast question* may also ask how something changes. For example, look at the following question:

8   Based on the article, how did Dorothea Lange's photography change after the Great Depression took place?

    F   She began photographing rich clients.

    G   She started using more expensive camera equipment.

    H   She focused on photographing the victims of the depression.

    J   She developed less expensive ways to develop her photographs.

This question asks about changes in Dorothea Lange's photography. Like many questions about change, this is really a type of *compare-and-contrast question*. It asks you to compare Dorothea's photography **before** the Great Depression with her photography **afterwards**.

Sometimes, it helps to make a Venn diagram to answer a *compare-and-contrast question*. To create a Venn diagram, start by drawing two overlapping circles, ovals or boxes. Then write down the characteristics common to the items you are comparing in the overlapping section. Put information unique to each item in the other part of each circle (*or other shape*).

The following page has a Venn diagram that could be used to answer this question:

BEFORE THE DEPRESSION   **DURING THE DEPRESSION**

- set up a studio in San Francisco
- primarily took portrait photographs

- took beautiful photographs
- lived in the West

- lost much of her business
- photographed people in bread lines
- took pictures of migrant workers
- captured the despair and determination of victims

Which answer best explains how Dorothea Lange's photography changed?

PRACTICE EXERCISE

Read the following poem by American poet Vachel Lindsay (1879–1931). He first achieved national recognition in 1913, when *Poetry Magazine* published one of his poems. Answer the questions on the next page after reading the poem.

The Flower-Fed Buffaloes

The flower-fed buffaloes of the spring
In the days of long ago,
Ranged where the locomotives sing
And the prairie flowers lie low;
The tossing, blooming, perfumed grass
Is swept away by wheat,
Wheels and wheels spin by
In the spring that still is sweet.
But the flower-fed buffaloes of the spring
Left us long ago
They gore no more, they bellow no more,
They trundle around the hills no more: —
With the Blackfeet lying low,
With the Pawnees lying low.

Vachel Lindsay

Blackfeet and Pawnees were Indian tribes on the Great Plains.

9 What is the main idea of the poem, "The Flower-fed Buffaloes"?

   A   Buffaloes still live in the same area as locomotives.
   B   In the spring, buffaloes enjoy eating prairie flowers.
   C   Buffaloes and Indians on the prairie have been lost to trains and wheat.
   D   The perfumed grass of the Great Plains brings prairie flowers.

10 Read this sentence from the poem.

   They trundle around the hills no more: —

In this sentence, "trundle" means to

   F   move around slowly   H   sleep in a special bed
   G   carry cargo   J   dig up the earth

11 Look at the following diagram which shows the sequence of events described in the poem.

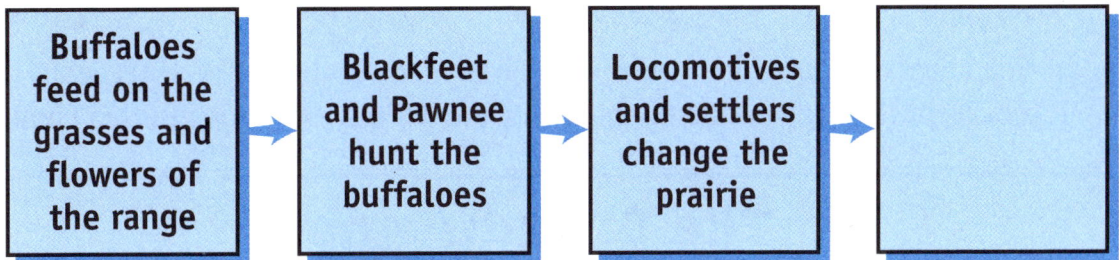

| Buffaloes feed on the grasses and flowers of the range | → | Blackfeet and Pawnee hunt the buffaloes | → | Locomotives and settlers change the prairie | → | |

Which of these best completes the diagram?

   A   Spring is the nicest time of the year.
   B   The Indian tribes of the prairie are numerous.
   C   The grass of the prairie has been replaced by wheat.
   D   In spring, the buffaloes eat the flowers on the prairie.

12 According to the poet, what led to the disappearance of the buffaloes?

   F   Indian tribes chased the buffaloes away.
   G   Buffaloes could not survive on wheat.
   H   Trains and settlers pushed the buffaloes off the prairie.
   J   Buffaloes moved to lands with better tasting flowers

13 How did life on the prairie change with the coming of locomotives?

   A   The number of buffaloes increased sharply.
   B   There were no longer buffaloes, Blackfeet or Pawnee.
   C   Buffaloes sometimes attacked trains.
   D   Buffaloes began to eat wheat instead of flowers.

CHAPTER 7

GOING BEYOND THE READING

Some questions on the **Grade 8 English Language Arts Test** will examine your ability to go beyond a basic understanding of the text. These questions will ask you to apply your background knowledge to make connections with the text. Such questions may ask you to:

- draw conclusions
- make predictions
- recognize an author's purpose
- recognize how a text is organized

In this chapter, you will learn how to answer such questions. First, read the following excerpt. It will provide the basis for the sample questions in this chapter.

The Breadwinner
by Deborah Ellis

The Breadwinner tells the story of Parvana, a young girl, and her family's struggle to survive under Taliban rule in Afghanistan. The Taliban have imposed strict rules on women and children — when they are outside, women must wear burqas (full length garments that cover them completely) and girls must wear chadors (head-and-shoulder coverings). Parvana's father supports his family as a letter reader and writer in the open-air market of Kabul. In this scene, Parvana sits behind her father in the maket.

"I can read that letter as well as Father can," Parvana whispered into the folds of her chador. "Well, almost." She didn't dare say those words out loud. The man beside her father would not want to hear her voice. Nor would anyone else in the Kabul market.

CONTINUED →

Parvana was there only to help her father walk to the market and back home after work. She sat well back on the blanket, her head and face covered by her *chador*. She wasn't supposed to be outside. The Taliban had ordered all the girls and women in Afghanistan to stay in their homes. They even forbade girls to go to school. Parvana had had to leave her sixth grade class, and her sister Nooria was not allowed to go to her high school. Their mother had been kicked out of her job at a radio station. For a year now, they had all been stuck inside one room, along with five-year-old Maryam and two-year-old Ali.

Parvana was always glad to go out, even though it meant sitting for hours on a blanket spread over the hard ground of the marketplace. At least it was something to do. She had even got used to holding her tongue and hiding her face.

She was small for her eleven years. As a small girl, she could usually get away with being outside without being questioned. "I need this girl to help me walk," her father would tell any Taliban supporter who asked, pointing to his leg. He had lost the lower part of his leg when the high school he was teaching in was bombed. His insides had been hurt somehow, too. He was often tired.

"I have no son at home, except for an infant," he would explain. Parvana would slump down further on the blanket to make herself look smaller. She was afraid to look up at the soldiers. She had seen what they did, especially to women, the way they would whip someone they thought should be punished. Sitting in the marketplace day after day, she had seen a lot. When the Taliban were around, what she wanted most of all was to be invisible.

Now the customer asked her father to read his letter again. "Read it slowly, so that I can remember it for my family." Paravana would have liked to get a letter. Mail delivery had recently started again in Afghanistan, after years of being disrupted by war. Many of her friends had fled the country. She thought they were in Pakistan, but she wasn't sure, so she couldn't write to them.

CONTINUED ➤

Her own family had moved so often because of the bombing her friends no longer knew where she was. "Afghans cover the earth like stars cover the sky," her father often said.

Her father finished reading the man's letter a second time. The customer thanked him and paid. "I will look for you when it is time to write a reply."

Most people in Afghanistan could not read or write. Parvana was one of the lucky ones. Both of her parents had been to university in England, and they believed in education for everyone, even girls.

The market was very busy. Men shopped for their families, and peddlers hawked their goods and services. Some, like the tea shop, had their own stalls. Tea boys ran back and forth in the marketplace, carrying tea to customers who couldn't leave their own shops, and then running back again with the empty cups.

"I could do that," Parvana whispered. She'd like to be able to run around in the market, to know its winding streets as well as she knew the walls of her home.

Her father turned to look at her. "I'd rather see you running around a school yard." He turned again to call out to the passing men. "Anything written! Anything read! Wonderful items for sale!"

Parvana frowned. It wasn't her fault she wasn't going to school! She would rather be there, too, instead of sitting on this uncomfortable blanket. She missed her friends, her blue and white school uniform, and doing things each day....

But now the country was ruled by the Taliban militia, and they had very definite ideas about how things should be run. When they first took over the capital city of Kabul and forbade girls to go to school, Parvana wasn't terribly unhappy. She had a test coming up in arithmetic that she hadn't prepared for, and she was in trouble for talking in class again. The teacher was going to send a note to her mother, but the Taliban took over first.

Now that you have finished the passage, let's look at the different kinds of questions that could be asked that go beyond the text itself.

DRAWING CONCLUSIONS

Some questions on the test may ask you to **draw conclusions** from details in the text. A *conclusion* is a general principle or judgment you can make based on details in the reading. To answer a conclusion question, you'll need to put on your "thinking cap" and use your own ability to reason.

Conclusion questions really stretch your thinking ability. In these kinds of questions, the answer will **not** be found directly in the reading. Instead, like a good detective, you need to look carefully at "clues" in the reading. These details or "clues" will point you to the correct answer.

To see how this works, pretend that you have an older brother. It was his turn to wash the dishes after dinner last night. Early this morning, you are awakened by your mother's voice. She is shouting that someone broke a dish and left its shattered pieces all over the floor of the kitchen.

EXPLAINING YOUR ANSWER

What conclusion would you draw? _____

_____

What led you to this conclusion? _____

_____

As you can see, *drawing a conclusion* requires you to go *beyond* the information you are given. You have to consider the details and see where they point to. No one told you that your brother broke the dish last night and failed to pick up the pieces. However, you can guess this is probably what happened.

Now let's look at a *conclusion question* about the story you just read.

1 What are Parvana's feelings about the Taliban government?

   A   She thinks they are the best government Afghanistan could have.

   B   She dislikes the restrictions they place on women and girls.

   C   She blames them for the bombing of her father's school.

   D   She agrees with the government that women should stay home.

The text does **not** directly tell us what Parvana thinks about the Taliban government. However, several details in the passage provide important clues:

★ Parvana would like to read letters with her father, but she cannot because of the Taliban's restrictions.

★ Parvana would like to go outside, more often, but she is forced to remain home under the Taliban's rules.

★ Parvana is afraid to look directly at Taliban soldiers.

★ When members of the Taliban are around, Parvana wants "to be invisible."

★ Parvana misses her school friends, but she is denied the right to attend school.

From these details you can conclude that Parvana is unhappy with the Taliban rule, and especially with the restrictions it has placed on Afghan women.

★ **Choice A** is wrong — the text provides no evidence that she thinks the Taliban provides good government.

★ **Choice C** is wrong because nothing in the text indicates that that she blames the Taliban for her father's injuries.

★ **Choice D** is wrong, since she misses school and does not agree that women should stay at home.

The evidence in the text leads to the conclusion that Parvana dislikes the Taliban restrictions on women. Therefore, the best answer is **choice B**.

To answer a *conclusion question*, you should take the following steps:

STRATEGIES FOR SUCCESS

First, read the question carefully. Does it ask you to draw a conclusion from the whole text or just a section of it?

Next, look over the choices. The central question you must ask yourself is: *Do details in the reading lead to any of the conclusions in the answer choices?*

★ Eliminate choices with conclusions that cannot be logically drawn from details in the reading; *and*

★ Eliminate choices that directly contradict something stated in the passage.

Finally, look back at the reading to see which of the remaining choices is correct. Apply your thinking skills to select the best answer.

Now let's try answering another *conclusion question*:

2 Which conclusion can **best** be drawn from this passage?

   F Parvana's family was better off when both her parents worked.
   G Parvana and her sisters prefer staying at home to going to school.
   H Women married to Taliban militia could work outside the home.
   J Most young Afghan women attended school until the Taliban took over.

PREDICTION QUESTIONS

Good readers try to predict what will happen next in the text. When you read, you should also try to make predictions or guess what will come next. Then see if your prediction comes true. Even when the story or informational passage reaches an end, you can still try to predict what might happen afterwards.

Prediction questions test your ability to apply what you have learned from the reading to new situations. *Prediction questions* might appear as follows:

What is most likely to happen next?	What is a character or person likely to do in a new situation?

For example, look at the following *prediction question*:

3   Based on the information from the passage, what would **most likely** happen if Parvana were caught outside her home without wearing her *chador*?

    A   She would be rewarded by the Taliban for her courage.
    B   She would be punished for violating the Taliban's rules.
    C   She would be excused since her father was injured.
    D   She would be given a job in the market selling tea.

EXPLAINING YOUR ANSWER

What is the answer? _____ Write the sentence(s) from the excerpt that you think supports your answer choice. _____

_____

_____

_____

_____

Based on the excerpt, choices A and D can quickly be eliminated. The Taliban have ordered all girls to stay at home and not to go outside without wearing a *chador*. Thus, it is unlikely that Parvana would be rewarded if she violates this rule. It is also unlikely that she would be given a job in the market. Parvana goes to the market to assist her father because he is injured. He has lost his teaching job under Taliban rule. From this, we can conclude that his injuries would receive no special treatment from the Taliban, and especially would not allow his daughter to violate Taliban rules about wearing a *chador*. Thus, choice C is also wrong. Choice B correctly predicts the most likely outcome — if Parvana went outside without a *chador*, she would probably be punished by the Taliban.

To answer a *prediction question*, follow this strategy:

STRATEGIES FOR SUCCESS

First, think about what you have learned from the text. Think about how the people or characters act and what they say.

> In this passage, the author has provided information about Taliban restrictions, and how they react when their rules are disobeyed.

Next, use what you have learned to predict what is most likely to happen next, or what is likely to happen in a new situation. The answer must be consistent with the information in the reading passage. Here is where you must apply your thinking skills. For example, if a character in a passage acts in a certain manner, we would expect that character to continue to act in the same way in a new situation.

> Here, the Taliban brutally punishes any woman who dares to violate its rules. In addition, the author has let the reader know how much Parvana fears the Taliban militia. From this, we can predict that it is most likely the Taliban would do the same and punish Parvana if she went outside without wearing her *chador*.

Finally, select the answer choice that is closest to your prediction.

AN AUTHOR'S PURPOSE

Understanding an author's purpose — why the author wrote the text — is often important to interpreting the meaning of the text. Some questions on the **Grade 8 English Language Arts Test** may ask you to identify an author's purpose. Such questions may ask you:

What is the purpose of the article?	What was the author's purpose in writing the text?	Why did the author most likely write the story?

Usually the author does not state his or her purpose directly. You have to use clues from the text to figure it out. Authors generally have one of the following purposes in mind when they write:

TO INFORM

Informational texts — such as articles about people, history or science — are usually written to provide readers with facts and ideas. Some informational texts describe people or events. Others may explain how something works, while still others teach readers about something or describe possible solutions to a problem.

TO ENTERTAIN

Literary texts are often written to entertain readers. Stories with interesting characters and lively plots are fun to read. However, literary works also often contain a lesson or moral. The author wants to communicate a general truth about life.

TO PERSUADE

Some authors write to persuade readers to form a particular opinion or to take a particular action. Letters to the editor, speeches, advertisements and essays are often written to persuade.

TO EXPRESS FEELINGS

Some authors write to express their deepest feelings or beliefs. The author wants to share an experience with readers. Personal stories, poems, and essays often express strong emotions.

A question about the purpose of the author of the excerpt from *The Breadwinner* might appear as follows:

4 The author most likely wrote this passage in order to

  F entertain readers with a humorous story
  G persuade readers to visit Afghanistan
  H propose a solution to Afghanistan's problems
  J illustrate life in Afghanistan under Taliban rule

EXPLAINING YOUR ANSWER

What is the answer? _____ What evidence from the text made you select that answer choice? _____

_____

_____

_____

Sometimes the author will state his or her purpose at the beginning or end of the passage. At other times, you must use clues from the text. This excerpt is a story, so you might think the author's purpose is just to entertain. However, the subject matter of the story is very serious. The main character, Parvana, fears the Taliban. We learn that they have changed her life in many ways — forced her from school, made her wear a *chador*, limited her movements outside the house, and restricted her parent's ability to earn a living. Nothing in this passage appears comical or funny.

Instead, the author is using a fictional character to show what it was like to live in Afghanistan under Taliban rule. We can guess that this description is based on the experiences of real people. There is nothing in the text that would support answer choices F, G, or H. Therefore, answer choice J is the best answer: the author's purpose seems to be to inform readers what it was like to live in Afghanistan under the rule of the Taliban.

To answer questions about the author's purpose, try adopting the strategy on the following page, often used by good readers:

STRATEGIES FOR SUCCESS

👑 **First**, read the selection carefully.

★ Look for clues to see what type of selection it is — for example, is it *informational*, *literary*, *persuasive* or *expressive*?

★ Try to think about **why** the author wrote the passage. Use clues from the passage to determine the author's intent.

🏰 **Next**, look over the answer choices. Often, these will include specific information about the reading.

★ Avoid answers that describe only one part of the selection.

★ Look for answers that refer to all of the reading accurately.

♞ **Finally**, select the answer choice that best identifies the author's purpose in writing the selection.

Look again at the poem "The Flower-fed Buffaloes" in the **Practice Exercise** of the last chapter (*page 66*). Then answer the following question:

5 The purpose of the poem is to

A   summarize the main events in the history of the prairie
B   express the poet's feelings about changes on the prairie
C   inform the reader how the buffaloes once lived
D   persuade the reader to combat environmental change

HOW THE TEXT IS ORGANIZED

Authors organize their writing in different ways, based on what they want to say. Here are just a few of the ways authors organize their writing:

★ **Chronological.** Authors tell about events in the order in which they happened.

★ **Descriptive.** Authors describe the qualities of a person, place, or thing — such as how a person looks or acts.

★ **Compare-and-Contrast.** Authors tell how two or more items are alike or different.

★ **Cause-and-Effect.** Authors give the causes of an event, describe the event, or tell about the effects of the event.

★ **Problem / Solution.** Authors describe a problem and then provide a possible solution.

Some questions on the test may ask you how information in a reading is organized. You have to use your knowledge of the ways that texts are organized to answer this kind of question.

In Chapter 6, you learned about *sequence*, *cause-and-effect*, and *compare-and-contrast questions*. The same key words that help you to identify these relationships can also help you determine how an author has organized a text. For example:

Type of Text	What to Look For
Chronological	The text describes a series of events and includes **key words** such as: *first, next, then, last,* and *finally*; or the text provides a series of times and dates.
Cause-and-Effect	The text has **key words** such as: *cause, effect, since, therefore, as a result*; or the text identifies events and then describes their causes and effects.
Compare-and-Contrast	The text describes two or more things and includes **key words** such as: *like, in contrast, similarly, in the same way, on the other hand,* or *one difference*.

Let's look at a sample question about the organization of a text. Read and answer the following question about the excerpt from *The Breadwinner*.

6   The author organizes the passage by

   F   listing ways that the Taliban were unfair to women

   G   describing a day at the market and a character's thoughts

   H   comparing the lifestyles of a father and daughter in Afghanistan

   J   retelling major events in the history of one Afghan family

Here is a strategy to help you answer this type of question:

STRATEGIES FOR SUCCESS

♛ **First**, when you read a selection, notice how the author has organized it. See if the author tells about events in the order in which they occur, describes a person or thing, compares items, gives causes and effects, or describes a problem and its solution.

> In this excerpt from *The Breadwinner*, the author describes events in the Kabul market. However, she often interrupts the description to give background information or to tell the reader Parvana's thoughts.

♜ **Then**, look at the question. Does it ask how the author organizes the ***entire reading*** or just a ***specific part*** of the reading? If it asks about a specific part of the reading, then re-read only those paragraphs.

♞ **Next**, look at the answer choices. You should notice that the answer choices may include details from the reading as well as different patterns of organization.

♛ **Finally**, select the answer choice that correctly identifies the method of textual organization and accurately describes any specific details from the reading.

Test your understanding of this type of question by answering a second question on the organization of the story in this chapter.

7   The author organizes the last four paragraphs of the passage by

    A   describing the reasons for Parvana's state of unhappiness
    B   blaming Parvana's problems on her wish to avoid a test
    C   presenting reasons why Parvana should accept life under the Taliban
    D   comparing Parvana's life with that of her father

EXPLAINING YOUR ANSWER

What is the answer? _____ What evidence from the text can you provide

to show that your answer is supported by material from the passage? _____

_____

CHAPTER 8

LITERARY ELEMENTS AND TECHNIQUES

Some questions on the **Grade 8 English Language Arts Test** will ask you about the elements of a literary text — setting, characters, plot, and theme. You may also be asked questions about literary techniques — the methods an author uses to achieve a particular effect on the reader.

LITERARY ELEMENTS

Before examining literary elements, first read the story below by one of the world's best short story writers, Guy de Maupassant (1850–1893). This story will provide a basis for the sample questions in this chapter.

THE PIECE OF STRING

Along all the roads around Goderville the peasants and their wives were coming to town for market day. The men moved with slow steps, their bodies bent forward. They were deformed by hard work and the weight of the plow. Some led a cow or a calf by a cord. Their wives, walking behind them, carried large baskets on their arms out of which chickens and ducks thrust their heads.

In the public square there was a crowd of people and animals. Mr. Hauchecome, a peasant from Breaute, had just arrived at Goderville and was directing his steps toward the square when he saw a piece of string on the ground. Mr. Hauchecome, economical like a true Norman, thought everything useful ought to be picked up.

Guy de Maupassant

CONTINUED

He bent down and took the bit of string from the ground when he noticed Mr. Malandain, the saddle maker, standing in his doorway looking at him. They had previously had business together and were on bad terms. Hauchecome was seized with shame to be seen by his enemy picking up a string out of the dirt.

He concealed his "find" under his shirt; then he pretended to be still looking on the ground for something valuable which he could not find. He then set off toward the market and was soon lost in the noisy crowd busy with endless bargaining. The peasants came and went, always in fear of being cheated.

Soon the square was deserted. At Jourdain's tavern, the great room was full of people eating. Suddenly a drum beat in the courtyard. The public crier called out: "It is hereby made known that there was lost this morning on the road to Benzeville a black leather wallet containing 500 francs.[1] The finder is requested to return the same to the mayor's office or to the owner, Mr. Houlbreque; there will be a twenty francs reward." Then the man went away.

Everyone began to discuss Mr. Houlbreque's chances of finding his wallet. They were finishing their coffee when the police chief appeared. He inquired: "Is Mr. Hauchecome of Breaute here?"

Hauchecome replied: "Here I am." The officer resumed: "Mr. Hauchecome, will you come with me to the mayor's office? The mayor would like to talk to you." The peasant, surprised and disturbed, rose and followed the policeman to the town hall.

The mayor, a stout man, was already waiting for him. "Mr. Hauchecome," he said, "you were seen this morning to pick up, on the road to Benzeville, the wallet lost by Mr. Houlbreque." Astounded, Hauchecome looked at the mayor, terrified by this strange suspicion of him.

[1]**franc** - a unit of French currency

CONTINUED

"Me pick up the wallet? Word of honor, I never heard of it."

"But you were seen by the saddle maker." The old man flushed with anger.

"Ah, he saw me pick up this string, Your Honor." Searching through his pocket, he drew out the piece of string. But the mayor, in disbelief, shook his head.

"You will not make me believe, Mr. Hauchecome, that Mr. Malandain, an honest man, mistook this string for a wallet."

The peasant, furious, lifted his hand to object, repeating: "It is the truth, the honest truth, Your Honor."

The mayor resumed: "After picking up the object, you stood looking for a long while in the mud to see if any money had fallen out."

The man choked with both anger and fear. "How can anyone tell such lies! How can anyone …. " There was no use in protesting; nobody believed him. He was soon confronted with Mr. Malandain, who repeated his testimony. At his own request, Hauchecome was searched; nothing was found on him. Finally the mayor discharged him with the warning that he would need to consult the prosecutor.

The news had spread. As he left the mayor's office, the old man was surrounded and questioned. He began to tell the story of the string. No one believed him. He went along, stopping his friends, showing his pockets turned inside out to prove he had nothing. They laughed at him. He grew distressed at not being believed, but knew not what to do. That evening, he took a turn in the village of Breaute in order to tell it to everybody. He only met with disbelief.

The next day a hired man in the employ of Mr. Breton returned the wallet and its contents to Mr. Houlbreque. The man claimed to have found the wallet in the road, but not knowing how to read, he gave it to his employer. The news spread through the neighborhood. Hauchecome immediately went around and began to recount his story in triumph: "What most grieved me was the lying. There is nothing so shameful as to be placed under a cloud on account of a lie."

CONTINUED

He talked of his adventure all day long. He stopped strangers to tell them. Yet something disturbed him without knowing exactly what it was. People had the air of joking while they listened. They did not seem convinced.

The next week he went to Jourdain's tavern. Malandain laughed on seeing him. When he was seated, he began to explain "the affair."

A horse dealer called to him: "Come, come, that's an old trick; I know all about your piece of string!"

Hauchecome stammered: "But the wallet was found." The man replied: "There is the one who finds and the one who reports. At any rate, you are mixed up in it." He understood. They accused him of having had the wallet returned by an accomplice. All at the table began to laugh. He went away in the midst of jeers.

He went home ashamed and choking with anger and confusion. His innocence seemed impossible to prove. Then he began to retell the adventure again, each time adding new reasons, his whole mind given up to the story of the string. He was believed even less as his defenses grew more complicated.

Hauchecome wasted away before their very eyes. His mind began to weaken. By the end of December, he took to his bed. He died in the first days of January. On his death bed he kept claiming his innocence, repeating: "*A piece of string, a piece of string — look — here it is, Mr. Mayor.*"

QUESTIONS ABOUT THE STORY SETTING

The setting of a story or other literary work is **where** and **when** it takes place. Many literary works have more than one setting. Remember that an author makes a choice in deciding where to set a literary work. Questions about the setting will often ask how the setting influences characters and events in the story. Some of these questions will focus on the **historical context** — how the beliefs and culture of the time in which the story takes place affect what happens. For example, look at the following question about the story "The Piece of String":

1   The story is set in a time and place in which people

    A   often gossip about one another   **C**   have little concern for money

    B   rarely meet except for business   **D**   are very trusting of outsiders

EXPLAINING YOUR ANSWER

What is the answer? _____ Write the sentence from the excerpt that you think best supports your answer. _____

_____

In this story, all the people are peasants or villagers. Their life is filled with the tedium of hard work. They live in a close-knit community where everybody knows each other. Lacking outside entertainment, they delight in gossip. Their gossip gives rise to the story. The other choices to this question are clearly wrong.

For questions about the setting of a story, try using the following approach:

STRATEGIES FOR SUCCESS

First, determine *where* and *when* the story takes place.
- ★ Descriptions of the setting are often found at the beginning of the story. Look for dates, references to events, and other similar clues. See if any of the places, people, or events correspond to an actual time or place you know about.
- ★ Also, remember that a story may be set in more than one location. Pay particular attention to changes in setting as the story unfolds.

Next, think about how the *time* and *place* of the story help make events in the story happen. Often, the central problem is shaped by the story's time and place. The author could choose to write about any place or time period. The author usually sets a story in a particular location and time for a reason. Think about the attitudes of the characters as well as the physical setting.

For example, "A Piece of String" is based on the attitudes and habits of French peasants in the nineteenth century. The story would be very different if it were set in present-day Manhattan.

Finally, look at the answer choices. Based on the question, select the one that best identifies the setting or explains how it affects events in the story.

QUESTIONS ABOUT THE CHARACTERS

Questions about the characters of a literary text may ask you the following:

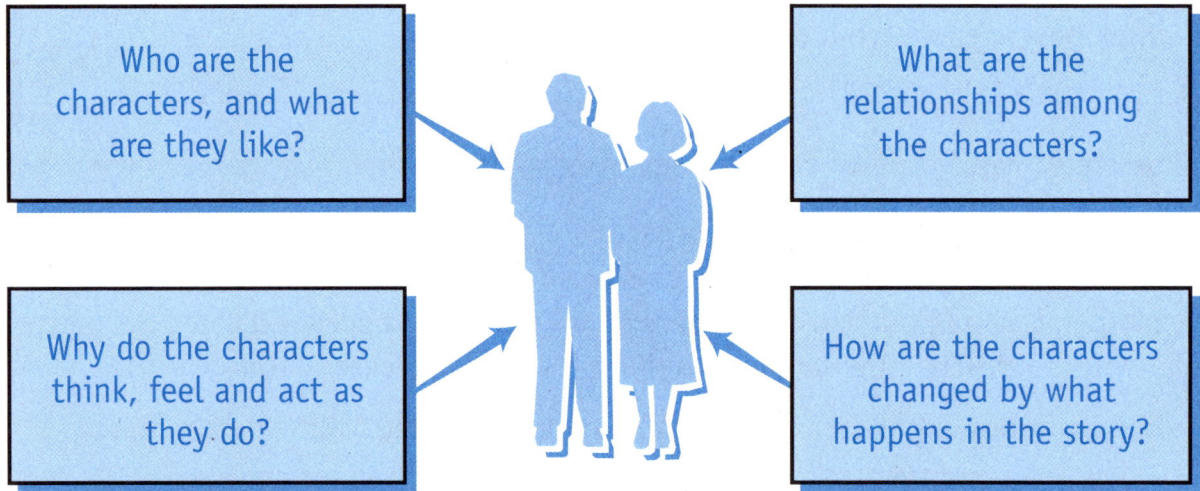

Who are the characters, and what are they like?	What are the relationships among the characters?
Why do the characters think, feel and act as they do?	How are the characters changed by what happens in the story?

Let's look at a sample question about a character in "The Piece of String."

2   Which pair of words **best** describes Hauchecome at the beginning of the story?

   F   honest and thrifty

   G   rude and snobbish

   H   angry and bitter

   J   suspicious and confused

EXPLAINING YOUR ANSWER

What is the answer? _____ What evidence from the text supports your answer choice? _____

_____

To answer this question, scan the text to find where Hauchecome is first described. Then see what details the author provides about him. In this case, Hauchecome is an "economical Norman" who thinks all things, even a discarded piece of string, should be picked up and used. Elsewhere in the story, we learn that Hauchecome becomes upset when people accuse him of dishonesty. Regarding choice G, H, and J, there is nothing in the text to support the view that Hauchecome is rude, angry, or suspicious at the beginning of the story.

To answer questions about the characters in a literary text, try these steps:

STRATEGIES FOR SUCCESS

First, remember that characters are usually described when they are first introduced in the story. It often helps to circle or underline the names of important characters when they are first mentioned. Then try to form a mental picture of what each character is like. Sometimes a character is not described directly: you have to decide what the character is like based on what the character *says* or *does*.

Next, read the question carefully to see what it is asking for.

Finally, **scan** the text to locate the details you need to answer the question.
- ★ If the question asks how a character *thinks* or *feels*, remember that you often have to decide what a character is thinking or feeling based on how the character acts.
- ★ If the question asks how a character is affected by an event, review the event carefully to see how the character is involved. Then compare what the character is like *before* and *after* the event.

Now, let's practice answering some additional questions about the characters in this story.

3 How is Hauchecome first affected by the news that the wallet has been returned?

    A He grows very ill.   **C** He becomes infuriated.

    B He feels triumphant.   **D** He is quite confused.

4 How are Hauchecome and Malandain alike?

    F Both suffer from the pains of old age.

    G Both have been falsely accused.

    H Both are farmers attending the market.

    J Both have a strong dislike for each other.

This is actually a form of compare-and-contrast question. First determine what the characters are like. Then compare their qualities.

WHO IS TELLING THE STORY?

Some questions on the **Grade 8 English Language Arts Test** may ask you to identify the **narrator** — the person who is telling the story. An author's choice of narrator is important for the way the story is seen by the reader. The narrator makes judgments, and gives or withholds information based on his or her own view of events.

Usually an author will use one of two ways to tell a story in a literary text:

★ **Outside Narrator.** One way of telling a story is by an all-knowing narrator — a kind of reporter who tells the story without being a character in it. The narrator tells the story in the **third person** — *he did this, she did that* – without using the pronoun "I." You can think of the narrator as sort of a camera recording what takes place for the reader. The narrator may or may not tell characters' inner thoughts.

★ **Story Character.** Sometimes one of the story characters actually "tells" the story. This could be the main character or one of the other characters. The narrator will use the pronoun "I" when describing his or her own actions. Here, the story-telling character can also express his or her own inner thoughts and feelings, but not those of other characters. Authors sometimes use this technique to make the story more interesting and realistic.

THE PLOT: CONFLICT AND RESOLUTION

The **plot** is what happens in the story. Usually, the main characters face some problem or conflict. This "conflict" could be the struggle of a character against nature, against another character, or an inner struggle within the character.

Some questions may ask you to identify the main conflict or problem in the passage. For example, look at this question dealing with "The Piece of String":

5   What is the main problem Hauchecome faces in the story?

   A   People believe he has dishonestly taken a lost wallet.
   B   The mayor of the town is annoyed with his conduct.
   C   The saddle maker and Hauchecome are on bad terms.
   D   He cannot find any use for a piece of string he has found.

EXPLAINING YOUR ANSWER

What is the answer? _____ Explain why you selected that answer. _____

_____

Although the saddle maker had a dispute with Hauchecome, that is not the central issue of the story. Likewise, we never learn that Hauchecome had a problem using the string he found. Finally, the mayor may have been annoyed with Hauchecome, but this again is just one small detail. It is not the central problem. **Choice A** is the best answer. People believe Hauchecome has found the lost wallet, despite his repeated denials. He speaks so much in his defense that people suspect he is covering up some dishonesty, even after the wallet is returned.

Other questions may ask you how the main conflict is resolved:

6   How is the problem faced by Hauchecome finally resolved?

    F   He becomes sick with anxiety and dies.

    G   He persuades the townspeople he is innocent.

    H   He is freed from suspicion when the wallet is found.

    J   He proves that Malandain could not see what he had picked up.

To answer these kinds of questions, you should take the following steps:

STRATEGIES FOR SUCCESS

First, read the story carefully to identify the main *problem* that the characters face. Usually this problem is presented early in the passage: it then drives most of the events in the story. The problem that ties together all of the events in "The Piece of String" is that Hauchecome is accused of lying about finding a lost wallet.

Next, think about how story events lead to a *resolution of this central problem or conflict*. In particular, look at how the story ends: how are things now different from the beginning of the story? In "The Piece of String," the fact that someone turns in the wallet might have resolved the problem, but it does not. Hauchecome keeps defending himself, and his efforts convince others that he is guilty. He then becomes consumed with anxiety and dies.

QUESTIONS ABOUT THE THEME

A **theme** is any underlying message, lesson or truth that a literary text expresses. It gives the text a universal significance. A literary work may have more than one theme. Sometimes a theme is mentioned directly in the story or poem. More often, you have to figure it out.

Here is a strategy used by many good readers to find the theme of a literary text:

STRATEGIES FOR SUCCESS

First, read the question carefully. A theme question may appear as:
★ *What is the theme of the story?*
★ *What lesson does a character learn in the story?*

Next, try to determine the general message of the story or poem. Think about the story's events. Then ask yourself: What lesson can I learn from this story? What advice does the author give to the reader? What universal truth does the story or poem demonstrate?

Finally, review the choices and select the one closest to the theme or lesson you have identified.

Let's see how well you can answer a question about the theme of a story.

7   What important lesson can the reader learn from this story?

   A   Even the humblest object can be put to good use.
   B   Villagers are usually more reliable than simple peasants.
   C   People suspect those who try too hard to prove their honesty.
   D   A person's standing in the community is often based on wealth.

EXPLAINING YOUR ANSWER

What is the answer? _____ Explain why you selected that answer. _____

_____

_____

LITERARY TECHNIQUES

Now let's look at **literary techniques** — those methods an author uses to achieve a particular effect on the reader.

QUESTIONS ABOUT THE TONE

Have you ever noticed that you can say the same thing with a different meaning by changing the tone of your voice? A written text can also have tone. **Tone** refers to the qualities of a passage that reveal an author's attitude toward its subject — the "mood" or flavor of the passage. The subject matter itself, the author's choice of words, sentence structures, expressions of feeling or opinion, punctuation and imagery all contribute to the *tone* of the passage.

Here are a few examples of different *tones* you might find a literary text:

★ A passage with a **factual** or **objective tone** is usually told by an "all-knowing," third-person narrator. Authors try to keep out all expressions of feeling or opinion, and try to appear impartial. Informational texts often have an objective tone.

★ To establish an **emotional** or **sentimental tone**, the author usually includes expressions of opinion and feeling. Such writing tends to show strong emotion, with colorful adjectives and verbs. The tone of an emotional text might be *angry*, *sad*, *regretful* or *joyful*. Often it is written in *first-person*.

★ A passage with a **humorous** or **comical tone** makes fun of the subject, either directly or indirectly. A humorous passage tries to make the reader laugh and usually has a happy ending.

★ In an **ironic** or **sarcastic** passage, the author presents things that often end up being the opposite of what might be expected. There is a contrast between what is said and what is meant.

Now that you know something about the **tone** of a literary work, look at the following question:

8   Which word **best** describes the tone of "The Piece of String"?

F   ironic   H   enthusiastic

G   sentimental   J   angry

EXPLAINING YOUR ANSWER

What is the answer? _____ What evidence from the text supports your answer choice? _____

_____

As you can see, a question about **tone** asks you to describe the mood of the passage. You have to evaluate the tone by looking at the subject matter, choice of words, expressions of opinion or feeling, imagery and other characteristics. Here, the tone is ironic because the author makes it clear that Hauchecome did not take the wallet. The narrator seems to report all this very objectively, although Hauchecome is described with emotion and the reactions of the townspeople are humorous.

To answer questions about **tone**, you should apply the following steps.

STRATEGIES FOR SUCCESS

The question will usually be phrased:
   ★ *What is the tone of the passage?*
   ★ *What phrase best describes the tone of the passage?*

First, look over the answer choices. Make sure that you understand the words used in each choice. Sometimes it is possible to eliminate choices you know are incorrect to arrive at the right answer.

Next, look over the passage. Consider the subject matter, the author's choice of words, length of sentences, expressions of feeling, and imagery. Does the writer seem impartial or state his or her opinions? What is the overall mood of the passage? Pick the answer closest to your own sense of the mood or flavor of the passage. Is the text objective, sad, happy, angry or humorous?

QUESTIONS ABOUT LITERARY DEVICES

Just as carpenters and other craftsmen use special techniques to construct a house, skilled writers use well-known devices to create works of literature. The test will examine your ability to read a literary selection and may ask you to identify the various devices that have been employed by the author to make it effective.

Before you can answer this kind of question, you should be familiar with some of the main literary devices used by authors:

GLOSSARY OF LITERARY DEVICES

❋ **Symbolism:** An author uses objects or events to suggest or represent something else. Authors use symbolism to give a deeper meaning to something. For example, the "rising sun" might be used by an author to symbolize a new start in a character's life.

❋ **Simile:** An author makes a comparison using "like" or "as." This gives one object the characteristics of another that is more familiar to us. For example: *The young child was as strong as an ox.*

❋ **Metaphor:** An author makes a comparison by stating one thing is another but without using "like" or "as." This again gives one object the characteristics of something else. For example: *She faces a sea of troubles.*

❋ **Personification:** An author gives human qualities, feelings, or characteristics to non-living objects. For example: *The rain kissed my face as it fell.*

❋ **Illustration:** An author explains a general point by providing a specific example.

❋ **Flashback:** An author interrupts the narrative of the story to go back to an earlier point in time, prior to the beginning of the story. Sometimes a character's recollection or a dream sequence is used for the flashback. The purpose of a flashback is to give background to the story.

❋ **Foreshadowing:** An author places an event in the story that foretells, resembles or provides some clue to what happens later.

Now that you know the chief literary devices, let's look at a sample question about how these devices can be used.

9 Which sentence from "The Piece of String" uses a metaphor?

   A "Soon the square was deserted."

   B "At any rate, you are mixed up in it."

   C "Everyone began to discuss Mr. Houlbreque's chances of finding his wallet."

   D "Astounded, Hauchecome looked at the mayor, terrified by the strange suspicion of him."

To answer this question, look at each answer choice to see which one is a metaphor. Remember that a **metaphor** applies the characteristics of one thing to describe something else without using *like* or *as*. Which of the answer choices does this? Since Hauchecome is not physically "mixed" in something, the language in choice B is a metaphor. Now try answering another question on literary devices.

10 Read this sentence from the story.

> *There is nothing so shameful as to be placed under a cloud on account of a lie.*

What writing technique does this sentence illustrate?

F metaphor
G foreshadowing
H personification
J symbolism

POETIC ELEMENTS

Poets make use of some special literary techniques. These include:

✳ **Repetition.** Poets repeat a particular word, phrase, or line of a poem. Poets also often repeat the same first consonant sounds — *soft skin* or *hard-hearted*. This technique is known as **alliteration**.

✳ **Rhythm.** Poets often use a pattern of syllables to create a beat or rhythm. For example, every other syllable might be emphasized:
> *"Twinkle, twinkle, little star."*

✳ **Rhyming Patterns.** Two words rhyme when they end in the same sound. Often poets rhyme different lines of a poem:

Ansel Adams was a picture taker,
His photos focused on mother nature.
With his camera in his hand,
He captured images of the land.

In this example, *taker* and *nature* rhyme, as do *hand* and *land*. Poets may rhyme every two lines, or every other line, or adopt any other rhyming pattern. Rhythm and rhyme give poetry its musical quality.

To answer a question about the use of literary devices, including poetic elements, try the strategy on the following page:

STRATEGIES FOR SUCCESS

How the Question Will Appear. This question will usually appear in one of two ways:

★ The question begins with a quotation from the reading passage and then asks you to identify the type of literary device it illustrates.

★ The question starts with the name of a literary device or poetic element, and then asks you to select a line from the passage that shows this technique.

Either way, this type of question basically asks you to match a literary device with an example of it from the reading. To answer it:

First, look at the question and determine what form it takes:

★ If the question starts with a quotation from the reading, go straight to the answer choices. Recall what each of the devices mentioned in the answer choice is and apply that knowledge to the quotation.

★ If it starts with the name of a literary device, recall what that is. For question 10 on the page 94, you should recall that a metaphor compares one thing to another without using **as** or **like**. The hardest part in answering this kind of question is remembering the different types of devices and poetic elements.

Finally, make the correct "match" between the literary device and the text. Decide which quotation best illustrates that type of device or which kind of literary device is illustrated by the quotation.

QUESTIONS ON THE AUTHOR'S USE OF LANGUAGE

The author of a poem, story or other literary text deliberately chooses language designed to arouse particular feelings in the reader. Some questions on the test may ask you to recognize how an author's use of language creates particular images or feelings. For example, look at the following question based on the passage, "The Piece of String":

11   Read this sentence from the story.

> **Astounded, Hauchecome looked at the mayor, terrified by this strange suspicion of him.**

With this description, the author creates a feeling of

A   jealousy   **C**   regret

B   surprise   **D**   triumph

EXPLAINING YOUR ANSWER

What is your answer? _____ Why did you select this answer? _____

_____

_____

To answer this kind of question, take the following steps:

STRATEGIES FOR SUCCESS

First, read the quotation in the question carefully. It often helps to scan the passage to find the context of the quotation.

Next, think about what the author has chosen to describe and the words the author has selected — especially adjectives, adverbs, and verbs to describe it. Based on the choices the author has made, what effect do you think the author was trying to create? Is the description sad, happy, dreamlike, frightening, or does it arouse some other emotion?

Finally, choose the answer that best identifies the feelings or images you experience when you read the quotation.

PRACTICE EXERCISE

Robert Frost (1874–1963) was a popular twentieth-century American poet. Read the following poem and then answer the questions that follow:

The Road Not Taken

1   Two roads diverged in a yellow wood,
2   And sorry I could not travel both
3   And be one traveler, long I stood
4   And looked down one as far as I could
5   To where it bent in the undergrowth;

6   Then took the other, as just as fair,
7   And having perhaps the better claim,
8   Because it was grassy and wanted wear;
9   Though as for that the passing there
10   Had worn them really about the same,

11   And both that morning equally lay
12   In leaves no step had trodden black.
13   Oh, I kept the first for another day!
14   Yet knowing how way leads on to way,
15   I doubted if I should ever come back.

16   I shall be telling this with a sigh
17   Somewhere ages and ages hence:
18   Two roads diverged in a wood, and I—
19   I took the one less traveled by,
20   And that has made all the difference.

12   The poem is told by

    F   a third-person narrator
    G   a traveler who walked in the woods
    H   a friend who witnessed the walk
    J   a person lost in the woods

13   Read this line from the poem:

    Two roads diverged in a yellow wood

In this line, "diverged" means the same thing as

    A   disagreed   **C**   separated
    B   departed   **D**   disappeared

14 In lines 13 through 15, the poet indicates that he

    F wants to leave the better road for his friends

    G hopes to take the other road one day but probably never will

    H believes the two roads will come back together

    J will take the other road some time later in the day

15 In the poem, the different roads probably symbolize

    A untamed nature   **C** different choices in life

    B contrasting periods of time   **D** the poet's typical day

16 The author most likely wrote this poem in order to

    F entertain readers with an amusing incident

    G persuade readers to go on more nature walks

    H explore the choices people make in life

    J show why some travelers like hiking

17 Which **best** describes the tone of the poem?

    A humorous   **C** thoughtful

    B informative   **D** sarcastic

18 What is the theme of the poem?

    F The best road to follow is the one traveled by others.

    G Life requires us to make choices.

    H People should recall choices that did not work out.

    J Travelers can be puzzled by too many choices.

19 Read these lines from the poem.

> *And having perhaps the better claim,*
> *Because it was grassy and wanted wear;*

What writing technique do these lines illustrate?

    A simile   **C** personification

    B foreshadowing   **D** illustration

20 How does the poet connect lines 1 and 18?

    F rhyme   **H** flashback

    G repetition   **J** metaphor

CHAPTER 9

EVALUATING INFORMATION

Some questions on the **Grade 8 English Language Arts Test** will examine your ability to analyze and evaluate information. These questions may ask you:

- to distinguish fact from opinion
- to consider an author's qualifications, biases, and viewpoint
- to evaluate the accuracy and validity of information
- to relate ideas and information
- to locate information

In this chapter, you will learn how to answer these kinds of questions. First, read the following article. It will provide the basis for the questions in this chapter.

ORANGUTANS HANG TOUGH
by Cheryl Knott

Dr. Cheryl Knott is a biological anthropologist and Assistant Professor of Anthropology at Harvard University. Her research focuses on how changes in the availability of food in the forest affect the behavior of orangutans. Dr. Knott has published widely on the subject of orangutan behavior.

"Marissa had a baby!" The good news arrived with my assistant Rhanda as he dashed into our research camp in Borneo's Gunung Palung National Park. For three days we hadn't seen Marissa, one of about 50 orangutans I've studied in the wild since 1994. Rhanda found Marissa eating fruit from a vine with the newborn female clinging to her mother's side. Orangutans bear young only about once every eight years (thought to be the longest span of any mammal), so there was much to celebrate.

CONTINUED

That was in 1998, shortly after I first reported on my research for National Geographic in several successive trips to Borneo. I've been relieved to find that Martina (as we named the new arrival) and the other orangutans at our site are doing quite well, despite the ever expanding reach of illegal logging.

But the threat of deforestation cannot be ignored. While our work continues to reveal new secrets about these apes, we're redoubling our efforts to protect their fragile habitat.

I and my team of field assistants have spent more than 50,000 hours over the past decade observing orangutan behavior and documenting the apes' physiology. Our work investigates how the boom-and-bust cycle of rain forest fruits affects

> Physiology= make-up, structure

the time between births and length of time children depend on their parents.

Recently we participated with other scientists to look at orangutan "culture" — customs passed from one generation to the next. These are often unique to particular populations. For example, Martina will grow up threatening strangers by making kiss-squeaking sounds into a handful of leaves — a behavior seen regularly only at our site.

A baby orangutan.

Some 500 miles west of Borneo in Sumatra, orangutans use sticks to pry calorie-rich seeds from thorny, hard-to-eat Nessia fruits, a clever trick that youngsters pick up from the adults — and one that Borneo's apes have not devised.

Another significant find at our site was that fully developed adult male orangutans, known as prime males, stay in top physical condition for only a few years. Following females and fighting with other males wears them down, diminishing masculine traits such as full cheek pads and large throat pouches and curbing certain behaviors like mating and long-calling — a loud bellowing made to announce their presence. As these features disappear, males become past their prime, a condition that usually signals the end of their reproductive life cycles.

Many orangutan males delay developing prime traits for several years, although they are still capable of fathering offspring. I believe the environment

CONTINUED ➔

may be partly responsible. Natural plant cycles cause severe changes in fruit production. During shortages orangutans consume fewer calories — and in females this translates to lower fertility. In response, males may wait to attain their prime condition until a time when food is more abundant and they have the best chance of reproducing.

Dr. Knott performs an experiment in Borneo

Sadly, the future looks bleak for orangutans. By some estimates more than 80 percent of all orangutans' habitat has been destroyed. Deforestation in Indonesia is escalating: since 1996 legal and illegal logging has consumed about five million acres of forest each year. Recent political upheaval has brought economic turmoil and lawlessness — hardly a recipe for successful conservation.

Populated with about 2,500 orangutans, Gunung Palung is one of their last strongholds. Overall orangutan numbers are falling. The 15,000 to 24,000 remaining apes could vanish within the next 20 years.

Meanwhile, Marissa, Martina, and the others here have much to teach us about how to ensure their survival. Through our educational programs and awareness campaigns, we are drawing attention to the orangutans' plight and helping to make a difference. It would be tragic to let these great apes slip away.

DISTINGUISHING FACT AND OPINION

Some questions on the **Grade 8 English Language Arts Test** may ask you to distinguish between *facts* and *opinions*.

★ A **fact** is a statement that can be checked or verified for accuracy. For example, the introduction to the article states that "*Dr. Cheryl Knott is a biological anthropologist and Assistant Professor of Anthropology at Harvard University.*" This is a statement of fact that can be checked.

★ An **opinion** is a statement of personal feelings or beliefs that cannot be checked for accuracy. Words such as *think*, *feel*, *probably*, and *believe* often show that a statement is an opinion. Value words, such as *best*, *great*, *wonderful* and *beautiful*, express personal judgments and are also opinions. For example, this sentence from the article — "I believe the environment may be partly responsible" — is an opinion held by Dr. Knott.

Much of what we read and hear is a mixture of fact and opinion. Writers often make statements that sound true but are really opinions. They do this to make themselves sound more convincing and authoritative.

Here is a strategy used by many good readers to help them distinguish factual statements from opinions.

STRATEGIES FOR SUCCESS

♛ **First**, read the question carefully to understand what it is asking for. Often, *fact-and-opinion questions* will appear as follows:
    ★ *Which statement from the article expresses an opinion?*
    ★ *Which excerpt from the passage expresses the author's opinion rather than a fact?*

♜ **Then** ask yourself: *Can this statement be checked, or is it an expression of the writer's beliefs?* Remember that facts can be shown to be correct or false, while opinions express a person's feelings.

Now let's see if you can answer a *fact-and-opinion question* based on the article "Orangutans Hang Tough."

1 Which statement from the article expresses an opinion?

    A "Marissa had a baby!"

    B "But the threat of deforestation cannot be ignored."

    C "Recently we participated with other scientists to look at orangutan 'culture.'"

    D "Overall, orangutan numbers are falling."

THE QUALIFICATIONS, BIASES, AND VIEWPOINTS OF THE AUTHOR

When you read an informational text, you usually seek to learn information about a topic. One important thing to consider is who has written the text:

★ Can you trust that the facts reported by the author are true?

★ Can you rely on the author's opinions?

Good readers often look at the qualifications and background of the author of an informational text. They consider the author's education, experience, and viewpoint to see if the statements can be trusted.

EDUCATION

In general, an author with specialized education or training relating to the subject of the article is more reliable than an author without such training. For example, Dr. Knott has special educational qualifications to write about orangutans. She has studied biological anthropology and is a professor at Harvard University, a leading American university. As a professor, her work is frequently reviewed by other professors in the same field, making it more reliable.

EXPERIENCE

Individuals with direct experience in the field they are writing about are generally more knowledgeable than authors lacking such experience. Often they are reporting events they have witnessed themselves, and their opinions are valuable because they have frequently considered the subject of their writing. In "Orangutans Hang Tough," Dr. Knott has had many experiences working with orangutans. This makes her text more reliable.

VIEWPOINT AND BIASES

If an author has something to gain by writing about the subject of the passage, then the reported information is less reliable because it may be one-sided. Even a highly educated or experienced author may have a special viewpoint or personal bias (*prejudice*) about the subject of the text. If the author has a special motive for persuading readers, the text becomes less reliable. When you read a text, you should therefore think about how the author's background may have shaped what the author chooses to include and leave out of the text.

On the test, you might be asked to determine an author's viewpoint from the text. This is similar to a detective investigating a crime scene. Authors often leave "clues" sprinkled throughout the text. Expressed opinions, the selection of facts, word choices, and descriptions can often tell you about the author's viewpoint. From this evidence, try to draw some conclusion about the author's views.

Now answer the question below about the article "Orangutans Hang Tough":

2   What **best** qualifies the author to write about orangutan behavior?

   F   She gives the views of groups opposed to logging.
   G   She is a strong supporter of protecting orangutans.
   H   She has spent many years in Borneo studying orangutans.
   J   She has lived in both Indonesia and the United States.

EXPLAINING YOUR ANSWER

What is the best answer? _____ Explain why you selected that answer. _____

_____

_____

To answer this kind of question, try these "moves":

STRATEGIES FOR SUCCESS

First, read the question carefully to understand what it is asking for. Such questions could appear as follows:
- ★ *What evidence indicates that the author is qualified?*
- ★ *What is the author's point of view?*
- ★ *How does the author's special background influence the text?*

Then, look at the passage for information about the author's education and experience. This may be presented in a separate introduction or in the text.

If the question asks about the author's viewpoint or bias, there should be information or clues in the passage to help you to determine this.
- ★ Consider both opinions and those facts that the author chooses to include.
- ★ Think how the author's viewpoint or bias may affect the reliability of the information in the passage.

EVALUATING THE ACCURACY AND VALIDITY OF INFORMATION

Some questions on the **Grade 8 English Language Arts Test** may ask you to evaluate whether the information presented in a text is accurate and valid. Information is **accurate** if it is true, while a statement is **valid** if its conclusions are logical. Three criteria generally help us determine the *accuracy* and *validity* of information presented in a text:

Is the source reliable?	Does the author provide factual support?	Is the reasoning logical?

RELIABILITY OF THE SOURCE

In the last section, you learned to consider education, experience and motives of an author. An impartial authority with specialized education and experience is generally likely to provide accurate and valid information. A source of information is also generally more reliable if it is published in a journal or other format with a history of making truthful and accurate statements. Often the editors of the journal check facts provided by the author before they publish the article.

You can better understand the reliability of a source by comparing the following two statements:

SURVEY # 1

A chewing gum manufacturer recently published the results of a study it conducted. The manufacturer found that in a survey of a thousand people who chew gum, its brand of gum was reported to have the best taste.

SURVEY # 2

A well-known independent consumer-testing organization released the results of a study it conducted. The report stated that a survey of one thousand consumers ranked the same chewing gum as the least tasty of five gums tested.

★ Which of these two statements do you think is more reliable?

★ How did you reach your conclusion?

FACTUAL SUPPORT

In an informational text, the author usually presents specific facts to support each major idea. Each fact can be checked by the reader. The more relevant facts the author presents, the more likely it is that the account is accurate and valid.

If the facts presented by the author contradict each other, it is less likely that the account is accurate. It is therefore important to check whether the different facts provided by an author conflict or agree. If the facts are **conflicting**, this means either that the account is incomplete, that the author has made a mistake, or that the author is deliberately trying to mislead the reader.

You should also consider if the author has presented *all* the relevant facts. For example, has the writer described *all* the causes of an event, *both* sides of a controversy, or *all* the steps in a process? Think of yourself as a lawyer, looking over the evidence presented by the writer. If key facts are conflicting or missing, then the account may not be reliable.

LOGICAL REASONING

To evaluate information in a text, consider the reasoning of the author. In logical reasoning, each step leads naturally to the next one. Every step is the logical conclusion of the previous step. An informational text is less likely to be valid and accurate if it contains any of these **logical fallacies** (*errors*):

LOGICAL FALLACIES

★ **Unsupported Generalizations.** General statements in the text lack factual support.

★ **False Analogies.** Analogies guide our thinking by comparing new situations with those we are familiar with. However, if the situations are not really similar, then the analogy is false.

★ **Irrelevant Information.** An author may attempt to persuade readers with information that has nothing to do with what the author is trying to show.

★ **Stating Opinions as Facts.** A statement may be misleadingly expressed in the form of a fact when it is really only an opinion.

★ **Oversimplification and Half Truths.** An argument is oversimplified when important details are left out. A text may provide information that is only partly true.

Try the strategy below to answer questions about the validity and accuracy of information in a text:

STRATEGIES FOR SUCCESS

Is the information logical and internally consistent?
If there are contradictions within the text, then the information becomes less believable. Each step in the author's discussion should lead logically to the next step.

Are the statements, conclusions and opinions supported by evidence?
Specific evidence can be checked for accuracy. Opinions and conclusions are more convincing when the author supports them with specific evidence.

Does the information in the reading agree with your own knowledge?
If what you read raises a question in your mind, then the account in the text may be inaccurate or incorrect. It is less likely to be true if it seems to go against your own prior knowledge and experience.

Does the author have any motive for making these statements?
If an author has some motive for persuading readers to believe something, then the information presented is suspect. Be sure the author provides specific evidence and logical reasoning.

Now try answering a question about the accuracy and validity of information in "Orangutans Hang Tough":

3 Information in the article appears accurate and valid because the author

    A   opposes the destruction of orangutan habitats by logging companies

    B   is highly qualified and reports events she has witnessed directly

    C   enjoys working with both young and old orangutans

    D   has the support of officials in Indonesia for her research

EXPLAINING YOUR ANSWER

What is the answer? _____ Explain your answer. _____

_____

_____

PERSUASIVE WRITING AND PROPAGANDA

In persuasive writing, an author generally provides logical reasons supported by specific examples and facts. However, advertisers and others who work at persuading people have discovered that people often act to satisfy their emotional needs. By appealing to the emotions of the reader, a writer may be more successful at convincing the reader than by appealing to reason alone.

Multiple Meanings. When evaluating texts designed to persuade readers — such as advertisements, political pamphlets, speeches, or posters — a reader should be aware that the text may actually have multiple meanings. First, there will be an apparent message — what is stated directly by the words of the text.

Then there may be an underlying or "hidden" agenda. This could be in the text or in pictures accompanying the text. For example, an advertisement may show a young couple driving in a car with their children. The words of the advertisement describe the dependability of the car. However, this advertisement has a hidden message — the car is so safe that people feel secure traveling in it with their children. Here, the hidden message appeals to the emotions of potential buyers.

Propaganda is a form of persuasive writing in which the government or a political group provides one-sided or biased information to win public support for its policies. Often propaganda makes use of logical fallacies and emotional appeals.

SOME TEST QUESTIONS MAY ASK YOU:

★ to distinguish between what a text or other type of communication actually says and its underlying message or hidden agenda.

★ to identify the techniques a communication uses to appeal to readers' emotions or beliefs.

★ to read a piece of propaganda and analyze how it tries to be convincing.

TO ANSWER THESE TYPES OF QUESTIONS:

■ Think about the purpose of the piece you are reading.

■ Use the same steps you would use to determine the *validity* and *accuracy* of a text.

■ Remember that some texts may have a hidden message.

■ Be aware of any emotional appeal or logical fallacy being used to persuade the reader.

RELATING IDEAS AND INFORMATION

Some questions on the test may examine your ability to relate ideas and details. You could be asked:

to find details to support a statement

to determine if information is relevant or irrelevant

to classify information

FINDING DETAILS TO SUPPORT A STATEMENT

Some questions may ask you which facts and details an author uses to support a particular idea. For example, read the following:

4 Which information from the article **best** shows that the birth of an orangutan is an unusual event?

    F   Illegal logging poses a threat to the survival of orangutan habitats.

    G   Orangutan females consume more calories when fruit is abundant.

    H   Orangutans typically give birth once every eight years.

    J   Dr. Knott and her colleagues have spent more than 50,000 hours studying orangutans.

EXPLAINING YOUR ANSWER

What is the answer? _____ Explain why you selected that answer choice.

_____

_____

For this kind of question, pretend you are a lawyer in court. You tell the jury: "Ladies and gentlemen of the jury, the birth of an orangutan is unusual." However, your opinion is **not** enough to persuade the jury. You must give *specific information* from the article to prove this general statement.

To answer this kind of question, here is one strategy used by good readers:

STRATEGIES FOR SUCCESS

First, read the question and make sure you understand what it says. Does the question ask you to find *facts*, *examples* or a *specific sentence* from the text?

Next, review the answer choices. Do any of the choices clearly support the general statement or idea in the question?

Finally, if you cannot answer the question after reading the choices, scan the text by looking for key words from the question. Read those sections of the text again. Then answer the question.

Now try answering a question on your own.

5   Which of the following information from the article **best** shows that orangutan behavior often differs from one location to another?

A   The author is a well-known biological anthropologist.
B   The sounds made by orangutans in some areas are unique.
C   On average, orangutans have children once every eight years.
D   Illegal logging is reducing the food available to orangutans.

RELEVANT AND IRRELEVANT INFORMATION

Some questions on the test may ask you to distinguish between relevant and irrelevant information. This kind of question usually asks you to relate details from the text to some outside idea or project. Information is **relevant** if it relates to a specific, defined purpose. If information cannot be used for this defined purpose — if it does not relate to that idea or goal — then it is **irrelevant**. Let's look at a sample question:

6   If you were writing a report about the origins of human culture, which fact from the passage would provide the **most** useful information?

F   Marissa the orangutan had a baby in 1998.
G   Scientists believe orangutans are able to teach their children.
H   Adult male orangutans remain in "prime" for only a few years.
J   Deforestation is destroying the orangutan's natural habitats.

To answer this question, here is the strategy you should use:

STRATEGIES FOR SUCCESS

First, look at the purpose the information is to be used for. For the question on the previous page, the information should relate to the origins of human culture.

Next, look at the facts or details in the answer choices. Go through each choice and decide if it can be used for the purpose identified in the question. Ask yourself:
Which of these specific facts relates to the topic or idea in the question?

In this question, the fact that Marissa had a baby would not explain anything about the origins of human culture. The same is true for choices H and J. However, the fact that orangutans can teach their children is relevant. It means there is some type of "orangutan culture." This would be useful for a report on the origins of human culture. This fact is ***relevant*** for that purpose.

Now that you know how to distinguish between relevant and irrelevant information, answer the following question on your own:

7 Which information from the article would be **least** useful to someone studying the child-bearing practices of different varieties of apes?

   A Logging is destroying orangutans' natural habitats.
   B When there is less fruit available, male orangutans delay having children.
   C Orangutans generally have children only once in eight years.
   D When an orangutan female has a child, it goes into hiding.

CLASSIFYING INFORMATION

A third way of relating ideas and facts is by classifying information. To **classify information**, group all the facts on the same topic together. It is often useful to classify individual facts to see if different facts about the same topic agree or contradict each other. For example, look back at the article. The general topic is Dr. Knott's work on orangutans. But there are several lesser sub-topics. These include the threat to the future survival of orangutans, orangutan child-bearing practices, and "orangutan culture."

A test question might ask you to *classify* facts by determining which of these sub-topics a particular fact belongs to. Look at the following question:

8 If you were classifying information, under which topic should you assign Dr. Knott's study of how fruit cycles affect orangutan births?

F the effects of deforestation   **H** "orangutan culture"
G male orangutan long-calling   **J** orangutan child-bearing

To answer this question, use the same approach you would for other questions relating facts and ideas. The key to answering this question is to decide which general idea Dr. Knott's study of fruit cycles and orangutan births most closely relates to. Then choose that topic as your answer.

LOCATING INFORMATION

Sometimes when you read, you may need to find out additional information. This could be information elsewhere in the same text or outside the text.

LOCATING INFORMATION IN A TEXT

Some questions on the **Grade 8 English Language Arts Test** may examine your ability to locate specific information within a text. Good readers use the *table of contents*, *index* and *glossary* to locate information inside a text.

TABLE OF CONTENTS

Books and magazines usually begin with a **table of contents** — a general guide that shows how the book is organized. Usually, the table of contents contains a list of chapters and the pages on which they can be found, like page *iv* of this book.

THE INDEX

An **index** is usually found at the back of a book. Unlike the table of contents, an index does not follow the order of the book. Instead, it lists every important subject in the book in alphabetical order, with the page numbers where that subject appears.

THE GLOSSARY

A **glossary** is sometimes found at the back of a book, especially a textbook. The glossary contains a list of key terms used in the book with their meanings. Often the glossary also provides the page number where each term is first defined.

LOCATING INFORMATION
OUTSIDE THE TEXT

You should also know where to find additional information outside a text.

★ **Reference Books.** You should know how to find information in a dictionary, encyclopedia, atlas, thesaurus, and almanac.

★ **Library Resources.** You should know how to use a computerized data base to locate books in your school or public library. **Fiction** is usually shelved by the last name of the author. **Biographies** are often shelved by the last name of the subject. Other **non-fiction** (*such as history, science, sports, and travel*) is shelved by a decimal number like 940.13, known as the "Dewey-decimal" number.

★ **Internet.** Information can often be found on the Internet by using a search engine like *Yahoo* or *Google*. When you read an article on the Internet, it often includes *links* to other websites with additional information on the same topic.

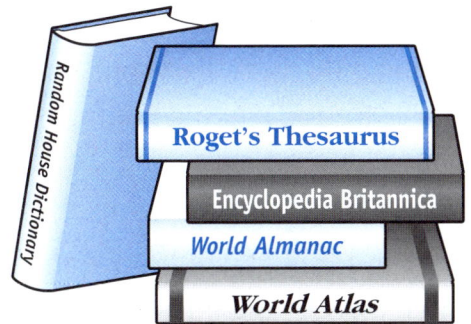

Now that you have some idea of how to find additional information, look at the following questions.

9 A reader is likely to find the **most** additional information about orangutan behavior by

  A looking up "orangutan" in a dictionary
  B using a search engine to look up "orangutan behavior" on the Internet
  C reading a biography of the former political leader of Borneo
  D examining a world atlas

10 Based on the article "Orangutans Hang Tough," in which library book would you **most likely** find additional information about Dr. Knott's research?

  F *International Journal of Animal Reproduction*
  G *Behavioral Responses of Orangutans in Borneo*
  H *Great and Small Apes of the World*
  J *A History of African Orangutans*

CHAPTER 10

A PRACTICE SESSION 1

The following pages have practice readings similar to those you will find on **Session 1** of the **Grade 8 English Language Arts Test**. Each passage is followed by a group of multiple-choice questions. On the actual test, there will be four to five reading passages and 26 multiple-choice questions. This practice test has three passages and 22 multiple-choice questions.

Read the article below about the work of noted social reformer Jane Addams. Then answer the questions that follow.

THE HOUSE THAT JANE BUILT

by Shawn Hoffelt

In 1877, seventeen-year-old Jane Addams entered Rockford Seminary in Illinois. At that time, Rockford graduates received certificates instead of college degrees. Determined to obtain a genuine college degree, Addams took advanced courses. She received her college diploma one year later.

After college, Addams traveled in Europe with Ellen Starr. Addams had become friends with Starr while they were students at Rockford. When she saw the dreadful conditions in which people lived in the slums of London, England, Addams' life commitment to social services began to take shape.

Jane Addams

Addams was inspired by the work done at Toynbee Hall, the world's first settlement house, located in an impoverished section of London. While visiting there, she observed college-educated people living in the community and helping to improve the lives of the needy.

CONTINUED ▶

Addams realized that her home state of Illinois had its share of poverty areas. In the city of Chicago, large numbers of immigrants lived in overcrowded and dirty conditions. Addams became convinced that to help the poor, she must know them first. She told Starr she wanted to establish a residence in which privileged young women would live and work among the poor of Chicago. Starr was enthusiastic, and the two women decided to turn Addams' idea into reality.

Addams and Starr searched Chicago for a big house that would suit their needs. They found a rundown mansion in a poor area of the city. With its spacious rooms and many fireplaces, the house had potential. All it needed was some cleaning and painting. Built by Charles Hull, a Chicago pioneer, the house was located in an immigrant community lean on resources, but rich in spirit and culture.

In September 1889, Addams and Starr moved into Hull House, Chicago's first settlement house. Addams knew that immigrants faced many difficulties. Few spoke English or understood American ways. They were unable to get work at anything but the most menial jobs. Entire families, including children, worked for pennies a day in factories. Few homes had indoor water or plumbing.

A class at Hull House

Addams and Starr began by helping wherever they were needed. They washed newborn babies, tended to the sick, and prepared the dead for burial. Addams worked alongside people in the community and gradually earned their respect. Addams and Starr gained recognition for their hard work and dedication.

Volunteers began to offer their services to Hull House. Programs that fit the needs of the community were launched. Classes to teach immigrants English and to assist the unemployed in their job searches were considered important. There were social activities for the elderly, as well as concerts and art shows at Hull House. A kindergarten and a playground were organized. Eventually, twelve buildings were added to Hull House, including a theatre, a gymnasium, a music school, a cafeteria, and a library.

CONTINUED

Hull House became a place of hope, offering its neighbors respect, support, and opportunity. Addams came to realize that the work at Hull House was as important to its volunteers as it was to the people of the community.

In the years that followed, the settlement house movement spread across the United States. Cities like New York and others modeled their settlement houses after Hull House. Jane Addams became known as "Our Nation's Defender of the Poor."

1   The author most likely wrote this passage

    A   to explain the origins and work of Hull House
    B   to entertain readers with an interesting story
    C   to tell how Jane Addams and Ellen Starr became friends
    D   to persuade readers to help the homeless

2   How were Toynbee Hall and Hull House similar?

    F   They were located in poor areas of London, England.
    G   They were established by American women.
    H   They placed college-educated volunteers with the needy.
    J   They were located near Rockford Seminary College.

3   Jane Addams purchased Hull House because it was located

    A   in a poor immigrant neighborhood
    B   near a wealthy suburb of Chicago
    C   close to the slums of London, England
    D   next to Rockford Seminary College

4   Which statement from the passage expresses an opinion?

    F   "After college, Addams traveled in Europe with Ellen Starr."
    G   "While visiting there, she observed college-educated people living in the community and helping to improve the lives of the needy."
    H   "Addams and Starr searched Chicago for a big house that would suit their needs."
    J   "Hull House became a place of hope, offering its neighbors respect, support, and opportunity."

5   Read this sentence from the passage:

> **They were unable to get work at anything but the most menial jobs.**

Which of the following would be considered a "menial" job?

A   doctor   C   dockyard worker
B   circus performer   D   school teacher

6   If you were writing a report about American education in the 1880s, which fact from the article would be **most** relevant?

F   Addams was inspired by Toynbee Hall in England.
G   Hull House provided classes to both children and adults.
H   Volunteers at Hull House helped mothers care for their babies.
J   Hull House was a former mansion in a poor area of the city.

7   The author would probably agree that

A   Addams' work helped to improve conditions for the poor
B   children require more attention than elderly people
C   too many immigrants came to the United States in the 1880s
D   slum conditions in London were worse than in Chicago

8   Which would be the **best** source to consult for additional information about Hull House?

F   a dictionary   H   a guidebook for Chicago
G   a biography of Jane Addams   J   a history of the United States

Chicago: 1905

National Archives

Read the following story by O. Henry. Then answer questions 9 to 16.

THE GIFT OF THE MAGI
by O. HENRY

One dollar and eighty-seven cents. That was all. And sixty cents of it was in pennies. Three times Della counted it. And the next day would be Christmas. There was nothing left to do but flop down on the couch and howl. So Della did it — sobs and sniffles, with sniffles predominating.

Her home consisted of a furnished flat at eight dollars per week. In the vestibule was a letter box with a card bearing the name "Mr. James Dillingham Young." The "Dillingham" had been flung to the breeze during a former period of prosperity when its possessor was being paid thirty dollars a week. Now the income was twenty dollars. But whenever Mr. James Dillingham Young came home he was called "Jim" and hugged by Mrs. James Dillingham Young, already introduced as Della.

Della finished her cry. Tomorrow would be Christmas Day and she had only $1.87 to buy a present for Jim. Her Jim. Many a happy hour she had spent planning for something nice for him. Something fine and rare and sterling — worthy of the honor of being owned by Jim.

Suddenly she whirled and looked at the mirror. Her eyes were shining brilliantly, but her face had lost its color within seconds. She pulled down her hair and let it fall to full length. Now, there were two possessions of the James Dillingham Youngs in which they both took pride. One was Jim's gold watch that had been his father's and grandfather's. The other was Della's hair.

So now Della's beautiful hair fell about her, reaching below her knee. She faltered for a minute and stood still while a tear splashed on the worn carpet. With a whirl and a brilliant sparkle in her eyes, she fluttered out the door and down the stairs to the street.

CONTINUED ➤

Where she stopped the sign read: "Mme. Sofronie. Hair Goods of All Kinds." One flight up Della ran, panting. "Madame Sofronie, will you buy my hair?" asked Della. "I buy hair" said Madame, and asked to see Della's. Down rippled the brown cascade.

"Twenty dollars," offered Madame, lifting the hair with a practiced hand. Della quickly took the money and let Madame cut her hair.

For the next two hours she was ransacking stores for Jim's present. She found it at last. It was a platinum chain simple in design. It was even worthy of *The Watch*. She bought it and hurried home.

When Della reached home she got out her curling iron to repair the ravages made by generosity and love. Within minutes her head was covered with curls that made her look like a schoolboy. She had a habit of saying silent prayers, and now whispered: "Please, make him think I am still pretty."

The door opened and Jim stepped inside. His eyes were fixed on Della, with an expression she couldn't read. It terrified her. It was not anger, nor surprise, nor disapproval, nor any sentiment she'd been prepared for. He simply stared at her fixedly with a peculiar expression on his face.

"Jim darling," she cried, "don't look at me that way. I had my hair cut and sold it because I couldn't live through Christmas without giving you a present. It'll grow out again. Jim, let's be happy. You don't know what a nice gift I have for you."

"You've cut off your hair?" he said with an air almost of idiocy.

"You needn't look for it," said Della. "It's sold and gone. Be good to me, for it went for you. Maybe the hairs on my head were numbered," she went on, "but nobody could ever count my love for you."

Out of his trance Jim drew a package from his overcoat pocket. "Don't make any mistake, Della," he said. "I don't think any haircut could make me like you any less. But if you'll unwrap that package, you may see why you had me going a while at first."

CONTINUED ➔

Her fingers tore at the paper. And a scream of joy; and then a quick change to hysterical tears. For there lay *The Combs* — the combs that Della had worshipped for so long in a Broadway window. Combs with jeweled rims — just the shade to wear in her beautiful vanished hair. She had yearned over them without any hope of possession. Now they were hers, but the hair that should have adorned them was gone. She hugged them to her chest, and said, "My hair grows so fast, Jim!"

Jim had not yet seen his beautiful present. She held it out to him eagerly. The precious metal flashed with a reflection of her bright and eager spirit. "Isn't it a dandy, Jim?" I hunted all over to find it. Give me your watch. I want to see how it looks on the chain." Instead of obeying, Jim fell to the couch and smiled.

"Della" he said, "let's put our presents away and keep them awhile. I sold the watch to get money to buy your combs."

The magi were wise men who brought gifts to the Babe (*Jesus*) in the manger. They invented the art of giving Christmas presents. Being wise, their gifts were no doubt wise ones. And here I have lamely related to you the uneventful chronicle of two foolish children of their house who most unwisely sacrificed for each other the greatest treasures. But in a last word to the wise, let it be said that of all who give gifts these two were the kindest. Of all who give and receive gifts, such as they are wisest. Everywhere they are wisest. They are the magi.

9   This story is mostly about how

    A   New Yorkers celebrated Christmas a century ago

    B   difficult it is to find just the right gift for someone

    C   beautiful hair can be just as valuable as a gold watch

    D   two people sacrificed their most valued possessions for each other

10   Read these sentences from the story:

> **So now Della's beautiful hair fell about her, reaching below her knee. She faltered for a minute and stood still while a tear splashed on the worn carpet.**

In this quotation, what does the word "faltered" mean?

    F   blamed   **H**   spun around

    G   hesitated   **J**   fell over

11 The story is told from the point of view of

    A Della

    B James

    C Madame Sofronie

    D a third-person narrator

12 Which pair of words best describes Della?

    F cold and unfeeling   **H** irrational and silly

    G loving and devoted   **J** depressed and inattentive

13 Why does Della let Madame Sonfronie cut her hair?

    A She thinks she will look better with shorter hair.

    B She needs money to buy a Christmas present.

    C She wants to wear combs that go best with short hair.

    D She believes her husband prefers her with shorter hair.

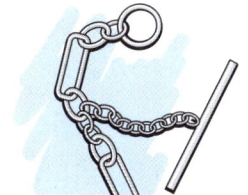

14 What is Jim's first reaction when he sees Della with short hair?

    F He is so stunned he falls into a trance.

    G He says he preferred her with long hair.

    H He breaks down into hysterical tears.

    J He tumbles down on the couch and smiles.

15 According to the story, why are Jim and Della the two "kindest" gift-givers of all?

    A They had no use for their new presents.

    B They spent time helping the needy.

    C They gave up what they most treasured out of love for each other.

    D They managed to live well on only twenty dollars a week.

16 Read these sentences from the story:

> **Tomorrow would be Christmas Day and she had only $1.87 to buy a present for Jim. Many a happy hour she had spent planning for something nice for him.**

In this description, the author creates a feeling of

    F anger   **H** comedy

    G sadness   **J** suspense

"We're All in the Telephone Book" is a poem written by Langston Hughes in 1947. Read the poem. Then answer questions 17 through 22.

WE'RE ALL IN THE TELEPHONE BOOK

We're all in the telephone book,
Folks from everywhere on earth —
Anderson to Zabrowski
It's a record of America's worth.

We're all in the telephone book.
There's no priority —
A millionaire like Rockefeller
Is likely to be behind me.

For generations men have dreamed
Of nations united as one.
Just look in your telephone book
To see where that dream's begun.

When Washington crossed the Delaware
And the pillars of tyranny shook,
He started the list of democracy
That's America's telephone book.

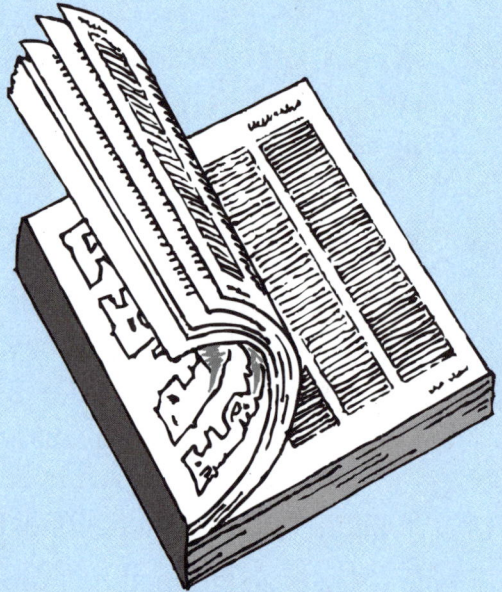

17   Read this line from the poem.

> **And the pillars of tyranny shook.**

Which literary device does this line illustrate?

A   flashback
B   foreshadowing
C   metaphor
D   alliteration

18   When the poet says "It's a record of America's worth," he means that the telephone book

F   provides a way to determine the wealth of Americans
G   lists all valuable American businesses
H   proves the value of American diversity
J   accurately portrays the financial value of the nation

19   What is the tone of the poem?

A   hopeful   C   tragic
B   objective   D   ironic

20   What does the telephone book symbolize?

F   the basic equality of Americans
G   the needs of American families
H   the different views of American citizens
J   the barriers separating different peoples

21   Which of the following pairs of lines from the poem rhymes?

A   For generations men have dreamed
    Of nations united as one
B   He started the list of democracy
    That's America's telephone book
C   We're all in the telephone book
    Anderson to Zabrowski
D   Folks from everywhere on earth —
    It's a record of America's worth

22   What is the main idea of the poem?

F   Washington started our democracy.
G   Many Americans are still not free.
H   American democracy is based on equality.
J   Americans come from many different lands.

SESSION 2:
LISTENING AND WRITING

Session 2 focuses on your listening and writing abilities. After your teacher reads a passage to you twice, you will be required to answer **three short-response** questions and **one extended-response** question. This unit will help you prepare for the listening and writing part of **Session 2**. You will practice listening and note-taking and learn how to answer short-response and extended-response questions.

CHAPTER 11

LISTENING AND NOTE-TAKING SKILLS

Do you know that you spend more time in school listening than reading? **Session 2** of the **Grade 8 English Language Arts Test** examines how carefully you listen.

DEVELOPING LISTENING SKILLS

Good listening requires active participation. It is not enough for you just to hear what is being said. Your mind has to be actively involved in listening. Focus on the voice of the speaker — voice, speed, emphasis, and pauses — to help you better understand the content of what is being said.

SOME PRE-TEST PRACTICE HINTS

Practice your listening skills by:

★ listening to story tapes from the library.

★ watching a television show without the sound. Look at the speaker's gestures. How do the gestures add meaning?

★ listening to stories read by a parent or friend. After listening, tell the speaker what you have understood about the story.

During **Session 2** of the test, your teacher will read an informational text aloud twice. Then you will answer both short-response and extended-response questions about that passage.

Some important steps for listening during **Session 2** of the test are:

★ **Get Ready.** Get ready to listen. Sit up straight. Face the teacher who is about to read the passage. Try not to think about other things as you focus on the passage you are about to hear.

★ **Focus on the Speaker.** Be prepared to pay special attention to any changes in voice that your teacher uses when reading the passage. Listen to pauses that give meaning to words. These are clues that will help you to better understand the passage.

★ **Listen for a Purpose.** As your teacher reads, you should concentrate on the *who*, *what*, *when*, *where*, *why*, and *how* of the listening passage. The passage may describe a person, tell about an event, explain an idea, or present new information. Be prepared to fill in a mental "graphic organizer" of these questions as the passage is read to you. Concentrate on the main idea and its most important supporting details.

The First Time the Passage is Read. Try to get an idea of its overall meaning. Attempt to "visualize" or "see" what's going on in the passage as it is being read. Think about what you already know about that topic. Create a mental picture of the events or ideas discussed in the passage. Ask yourself any questions you may have about the passage. Make predictions of what you think will happen.

The Second Time the Passage is Read. Focus on the details of the passage. What ideas, examples, and factual details does the author provide? Listen carefully to any words or sentences you did not hear or understand the first time the passage was read. Answer any questions you may have about the passage.

DEVELOPING NOTE-TAKING SKILLS

As your teacher reads the passage, it's important for you to take notes. Note-taking will help you to keep track of the ideas and details in the listening passage. Note-taking also helps you to keep focused on what the speaker is saying.

Here are three methods of taking notes. Make a copy of one of these formats on a separate sheet of paper. Then fill in the missing information as you listen to the practice passage, "Starting a New Life," being read by your teacher.

MAIN IDEA AND SUPPORTING DETAILS

This format is useful for a listening passage that describes or explains something, or that presents a list of arguments or reasons.

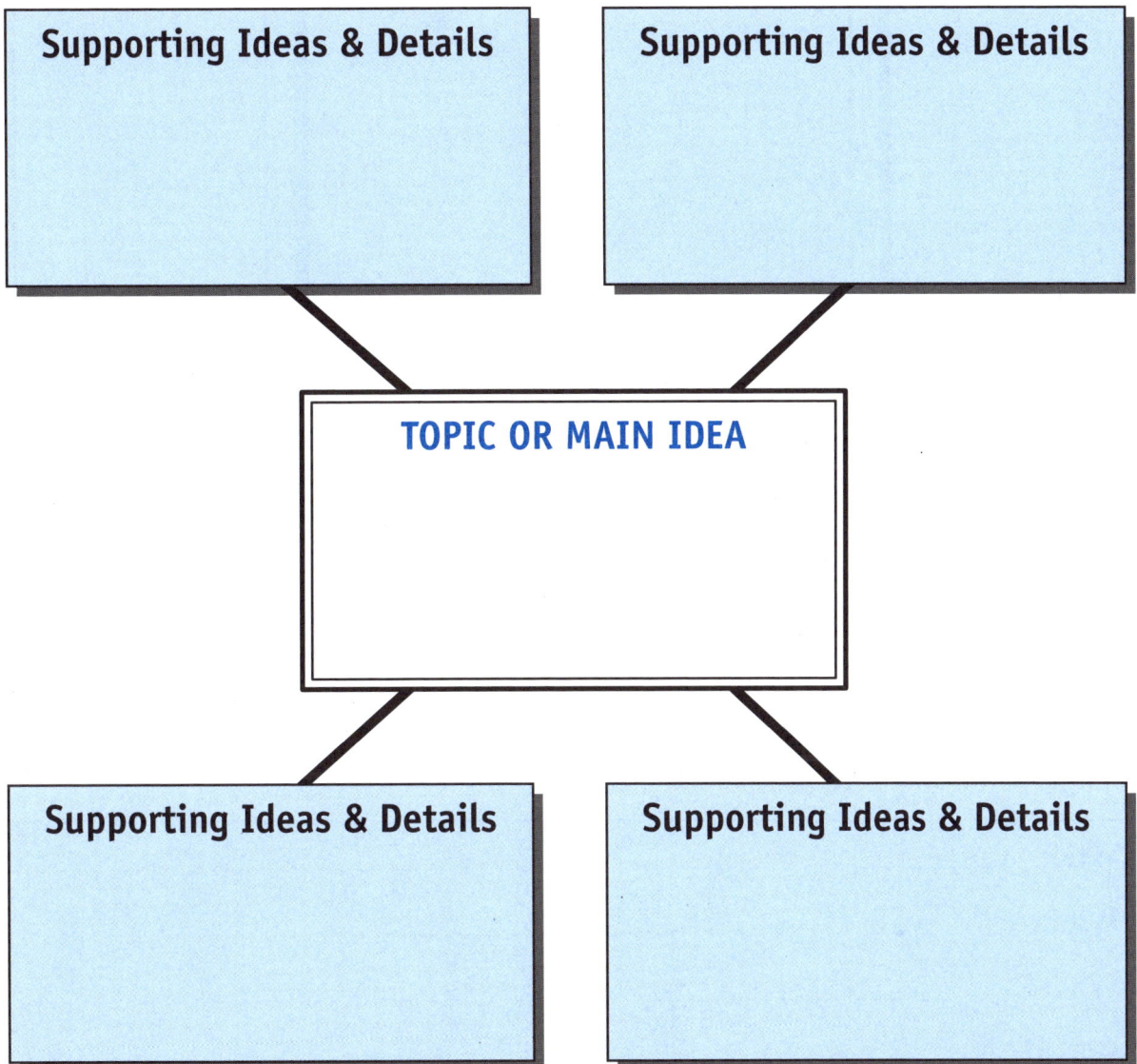

Supporting Ideas & Details	**Supporting Ideas & Details**

TOPIC OR MAIN IDEA

Supporting Ideas & Details	**Supporting Ideas & Details**

You may need to listen to the passage before you fully grasp its main idea. Mark the topic or main idea *after* you have heard the passage once. Change it if you need to after you have listened to the passage a second time. Think about the key question words *who*, *what*, *when*, *where*, *how* and *why* as you fill in the supporting details.

TIMELINE OR SEQUENCE MAP

If the listening passage describes an event or series of events, you may want to create a timeline or sequence map with the most important details. If this should be the case, here is a format that lends itself to better note-taking:

EVENT: _____

QUESTION WORD FORMAT

A final way to take notes as you listen to a text is to jot down the answers to the six major question words. This format is best for describing an event or action. Here is a suggested format for this method:

Who: _____

What: _____

Where: _____

When: _____

How: _____

Why: _____

PRACTICE EXERCISE

Listening and note-taking are skills that improve with practice. You should practice listening to stories and newspaper articles that someone else reads aloud. Ask a teacher, parent or friend to read the passage "Starting a New Life" by Jasmina Hamidovic (*page 202*) to you twice. Use one of the note-taking forms you just read about on the previous two pages. On a separate sheet of paper, take notes as you listen to the passage.

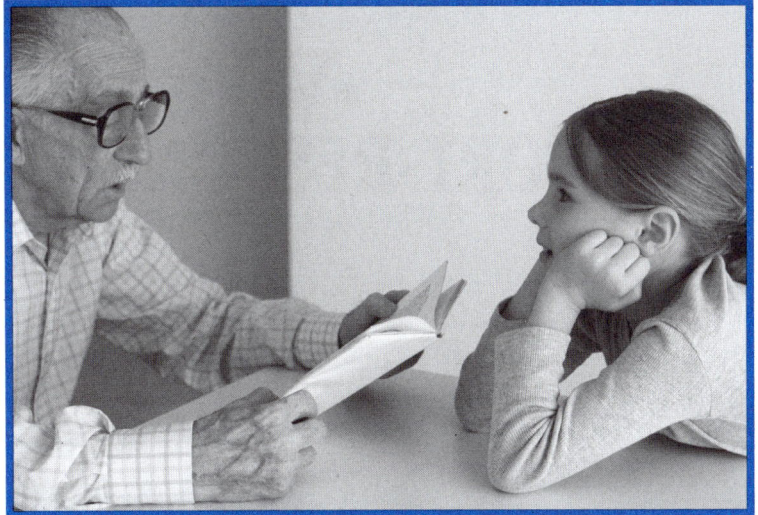

Listening is a skill that improves with practice.

DURING THE FIRST READING

The first time the passage is read, listen to get an overall idea of what it is about, and take some notes. Practice using the techniques for listening and note-taking you just learned in this chapter.

DURING THE SECOND READING

The second time the passage is read, continue filling in your note-taking form. Complete the form after the reading is over. When you are finished with your note-taking, ask yourself:

★ Did you correctly record all the elements of the listening passage — its topic, main idea and most important supporting details?

★ Is there anything important that you left out?

After you are satisfied with your notes, compare them with the model notes on the bottom of page 202.

CHAPTER 12

ANSWERING SHORT-RESPONSE QUESTIONS

Unlike multiple-choice questions, short-response questions ask you to do more than just select the correct answer. A short-response question requires you to write out the correct answer yourself.

★ In **Session 2**, three questions will require you to write short responses based on the listening passage.

★ In **Session 3**, you will also be asked to answer three short-response questions based on paired reading passages.

This chapter will examine the different ways these questions might be asked and show you how to write your answer.

FOCUS ON THE PASSAGE

Many short-response questions will focus on your basic understanding of the listening or reading passage. Some questions may ask you to complete the answer in a graphic organizer. You may not always have to write out your answer in complete sentences. The question might just ask you for a name or phrase from the passage.

Very often, the answer will be stated directly in the listening or reading passage. This means the answer will be spoken when the story is read aloud or stated directly in the written text. Therefore, you must pay careful attention to what you listen to or read.

You should be sure to base your answer on information from the passage. To write your response, you will therefore have to remember important ideas and details from the text. This is where your notes can be especially helpful.

★ During **Session 2**, you may check your notes to find the answer.

★ During **Session 3**, you may scan the text to find information for your answer.

After you have finished writing your answer, you should look back at the question. Ask yourself whether you have completely answered the question with specific information from the listening or reading passage.

THE MEANING OF QUESTION WORDS

A short-response question will usually ask you about the **what**, **how** or **why** of the passage. It may even ask for your **opinion** about something in the passage. The question words — *what*, *how*, and *why* — provide the keys to what you are expected to do. Let's look more closely at what each of these question words means.

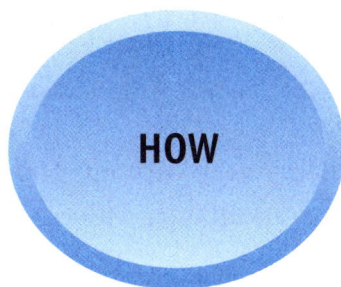

WHAT	HOW	WHY

"WHAT" QUESTIONS

"What" questions usually ask you to *identify* or *explain* specific things mentioned in the passage. For example, this type of question might ask you to identify the main idea of the passage or important details.

"What" questions about details can be phrased in a variety of ways. Here is a question that could be asked about the passage "Starting A New Life" by Jasmina Hamidovic which you listened to at the end of the last chapter. You can review the passage on page 202.

> **What were some of the challenges Jasmina faced in the United States?**

To answer a "what" question, you will usually have to recall specific information from the listening passage. In this case, the passage described some of the challenges Jasmina faced in America. For example, she had to learn an entirely new language and adjust to a new environment in school.

Another question about details from the same listening passage might ask:

What happened when Jasmina moved to Zagreb?

A "what" question may sometimes ask you to go beyond what is directly stated in the story or article. You might be asked:

to identify the main idea	**to draw a conclusion**	**to identify effects**	**to state a lesson you learned from the passage**

Frequently, such questions will ask you to provide one or more details from the listening or reading passage to support your answer. Here is what the question would be like:

CHECKING YOUR UNDERSTANDING

What is the main idea of the listening passage, "Starting a New Life"? Provide details from the article to support your answer.

_____

_____

_____

_____

_____

The following page describes some of the strategies you can use to answer a "what" question.

STRATEGIES FOR SUCCESS

First, look at the question carefully. See *what* the question asks for.
  * ★ Does the question ask for a **detail** that was stated directly in the article?
  * ★ Does the question ask for a **main idea**, **conclusion**, **prediction** or **lesson**?

Next, see if you can remember the details the question asks about:
  * ★ During **Session 2**, look over your notes. These should help you to recall the correct answer.
  * ★ During **Session 3**, **scan** the text of the passage to find the information you need to answer the question.
  * ★ If the question asks for a **lesson** or **conclusion**, think about what you can conclude from what happens in the passage.

Finally, write your answer in the space provided. Sometimes you will only need to write a few words or to complete a graphic organizer.

Now you try answering another "what" question:

CHECKING YOUR UNDERSTANDING

What were some of the things Jasmina liked most about her new country?

_____

_____

"HOW" QUESTIONS

"**How**" simply means "in what way." A "how" question might ask you to tell the way in which something in the passage is done. For example:

How did Jasmina react when she first came to the United States?

A "how" question might also ask about the way in which an event has taken place or a person in the text has changed. Here is another example of a "how" question:

CHECKING YOUR UNDERSTANDING

How did Jasmina's life change after Bosnia was invaded?
Provide details from the article to support your answer.

_____

_____

_____

_____

To answer this question, you have to recall details from the listening passage. You would need to remember that:

★ People from Serbia invaded Bosnia.

★ Jasmina's parents lost their jobs, and soldiers took over their house.

★ Life in Bosnia for Jasmina and her family became unsafe.

A "how" question may also ask you to compare different details from the passage. You could be asked to describe ***how*** two people or events are different or alike. For example, you might be asked the following:

CHECKING YOUR UNDERSTANDING

Explain how life for Jasmina in America was different
from her life in Bosnia.

_____

_____

_____

_____

Following are some strategies used by good readers when they are asked to answer a "how" question:

STRATEGIES FOR SUCCESS

The question word **"how"** often relates to a series of actions or events. In this case, your task is to show the ways in which these actions or events are connected. To do this, describe each separate event and show the way in which these events fit together to explain the whole.

To show **"how"** a person or situation changes, describe that person or situation at the start of the passage. Then describe what this person or situation is like later in the passage after the change has occurred.

To show **"how"** two people, events or situations are **alike** or **different**, here are some guidelines to follow:
- ★ To show how two people or things are *alike*, point out their similarities.
  In both Bosnia and the United States, Jasmina attended school.
- ★ To show how two people or situations are *different*, identify what is true of each one but not both of them.
  With the coming of the war in Bosnia, Jasmina no longer felt safe. In America, she felt safer than she had expected.

Now try answering the following "how" question:

CHECKING YOUR UNDERSTANDING

How did Jasmina think American schools compared to the schools in Bosnia? Provide details from the article to support your answer.

_____

_____

_____

_____

"WHY" QUESTIONS

"Why" questions focus on causes. They ask you to give one or more reasons *why* something took place. Often a "why" question asks you to tell about the motives or reasons that led a person or group of people to do something. To understand this type of question, look at the following "why" question:

CHECKING YOUR UNDERSTANDING

Why did Jasmina's family decide to come to the United States?

_____

_____

_____

To answer this question, you have to think about the reasons "**why**" Jasmina's family decided to leave their home in Bosnia and come to the United States. Let's review some of the reasons that were stated in the listening passage:

★ When Bosnia was invaded, the family felt unsafe because they were Muslim.

★ Jasmina's mother and father were fired from their jobs.

★ Soldiers took over their home and forced them out.

★ The family felt insecure about living in Bosnia.

Don't Be Fooled!

Not every short-answer question will appear exactly as you see them in this chapter. Sometimes the *same question* may be asked *differently*. For example, a "**why**" question might be disguised as a "**what**" question:

What reasons led Jasmina's family to leave Bosnia?

This may look like a "what" question, but it is really a "why" question for the purposes of this chapter. It is actually asking for the *causes* of something.

When answering "why" questions, here are some steps you might wish to apply:

STRATEGIES FOR SUCCESS

♛ Look carefully at the question. Decide which event in the passage you are being asked to explain.

♜ Think about what things in the story *caused* this event to happen. Often, the reasons for the event will be stated directly in the passage.

★ During **Session 2**, check your notes to review details in the passage if you cannot remember them.

★ During **Session 3**, scan the reading passage to find information that could be used to answer the question.

♞ If the question asks *why* a person did something, think about what the person wanted to achieve and the actions he or she took to reach these goals.

♛ After you have completed your response, check your answer to see that you have *fully* answered the question with information from the listening or reading passage.

Let's see how well you can apply these steps to answering a "why" question.

CHECKING YOUR UNDERSTANDING

Why did Jasmina watch American television programs while living in Zagreb? Provide details from the article to support your answer.

_____

_____

_____

COMPLETING GRAPHIC ORGANIZERS

A **graphic organizer** presents information in boxes, circles or some other form. A short-response question may ask you to fill in these shapes with details from the listening or reading passage.

For example, you might be asked to complete one of the following:

| Web or Concept Map | Timeline or Sequence Map | Chart or Venn Diagram |

These questions often do not ask you to write complete sentences. Usually, you will only have to write a few names or words in the empty spaces. Let's take a closer look at the different types of graphic-organizer questions you could be asked to complete.

A WEB OR CONCEPT MAP

A **web** or **concept map** places a topic from the passage in the center of the organizer. This topic is then surrounded with supporting examples, facts or details from the passage. This type of graphic organizer is often used to describe an idea, person, place or event. Complete the concept map below by answering the following question about the passage "Starting a New Life."

Using information from the passage, fill in the web with three characteristics of Jasmina's new life in the United States.

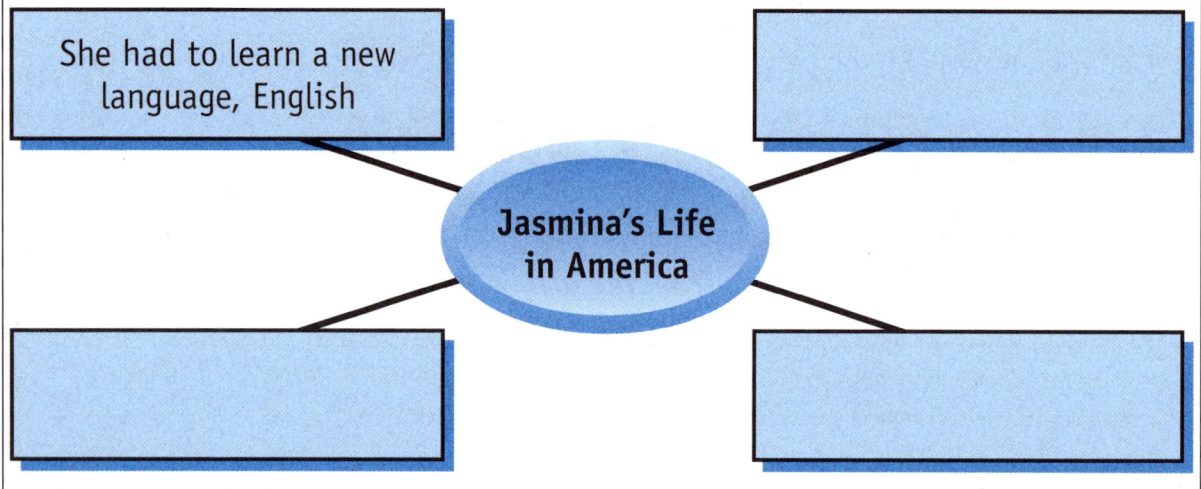

She had to learn a new language, English

Jasmina's Life in America

A TIMELINE OR SEQUENCE MAP

A **timeline** or **sequence map** traces how a series of events has developed over time. A *timeline question* asks you to identify missing events in the order in which they occurred. Complete the sequence map on the next page about the same passage:

Fill in the sequence map with three key events in Jasmina's life.

Serbian soldiers invade Jasmina's home in Bosnia.	→		→		→	

CHARTS AND VENN DIAGRAMS

A **chart** is a display of information, usually arranged in columns and rows. A **Venn diagram** is a chart of overlapping shapes used for comparing things. Complete the chart below with information from the listening passage.

Using information from the passage, fill in the chart comparing Jasmina's life in Bosnia and America.

	Life in Bosnia	Life in America
Security		
Religion		
School		

See pages 65 to 66 for more about Venn diagrams

HOW YOUR ANSWER WILL BE SCORED

Your short responses will be scored together with your extended response for each session of the test. In order to get the highest possible score, be sure to provide the specific information that the question asks for. This means that you need to include specific examples and other supporting details from the listening or reading passage to answer the question.

The information that you provide should be clear and be connected in some way to the passage. If you include any information beyond what is in the text of the passage in your answer, be sure it is directly linked to the task in the question.

★ If your answer includes some correct information, but most of your response is too general, incomplete, or partly incorrect, you will only receive partial credit for your answer.

★ If your answer is completely inaccurate, confused, or does not relate to the question, you may receive no credit at all (0 points). This will reduce your total "cluster" score.

PRACTICE EXERCISE

Have your teacher, parent or friend read aloud the passage to you "Keeping Time in a Timeless Place," found on page 203. Use this passage to practice your listening skills. Then answer the following questions:

1 Using information from the article, fill in the web below with three facts about the Palace of Versailles.

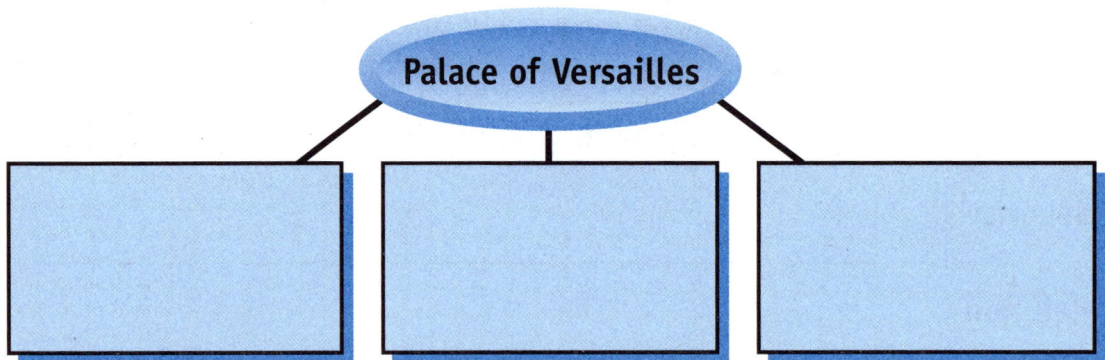

Palace of Versailles

2 What are two of Mr. Draux's responsibilities at the Palace of Versailles? Use details from the article to support your answer.

1. _____

2. _____

3 Using information from the article, fill in the chart with two reasons why many French people still support traditional crafts.

	Reasons to Support Traditional Crafts
1	
2	

CHAPTER 13

ANSWERING EXTENDED-RESPONSE QUESTIONS

In addition to asking you to answer short-response questions, both **Session 2** and **Session 3** will each require you to answer one **extended-response question**. An extended-response question will always require a written answer of one or more paragraphs. Here is an example of an extended-response question based on the listening passage "Keeping Time in a Timeless Place," which you heard at the end of the last chapter. If you need to, you can read the text of that passage on page 203.

> The author of the article writes that Mr. Draux's work at the Versailles Palace shows the support France gives to traditional skills. Explain how Mr. Draux's work shows this, and give your opinion on whether this is a good thing. Use details from the article to support your answer.
>
> In your answer be sure to include
>
> - what Mr. Draux does at Versailles
> - how this illustrates French support for traditional skills
> - whether you think such support is a good idea
> - details from the article to explain your opinion

Check your writing for correct spelling, grammar, and punctuation.

Unlike a short-response answer, your extended-response will receive two separate scores:

★ **Response to the Question:** Your extended-response will be scored with your short answers as part of a "cluster." This score will be based on how well you answer the question and support your answer with details from the listening or reading passage.

★ **Writing Conventions:** You will receive a separate score for how well your extended-response answer follows standard writing conventions.

MODEL STUDENT ANSWERS

As you can see, your extended response for each session will be scored along with your short responses as one complete "cluster." Together, your four answers on each session will receive a score of 0 to 5 points. This score will be based on how well you answer all four questions.

★ **No Points.** A score of "**0**" is the lowest score. It basically means the student has not answered the question at all. The response is either incorrect, unrelated to the question, or hard to understand.

★ **Five Points.** A score of "**5**" is the highest score. It means the student has completely answered the question and the response is well supported with details and examples from the passage. Moreover, the student has organized and expressed these ideas and details well, and has made some relevant connections beyond the text.

It often helps to read other student responses to see how well they have answered the same extended-response question. The question on page 141 was given to a class of eighth-grade students. After you read each student response, give it a score. You can see the complete rubric on page 201.

STUDENT RESPONSE A:

Mr. Draux is in charge of the antique clocks at the Versailles Palace in France. When the palace is closed to visitors, he travels around the palace. He goes from room to room to check the time and fix any broken clocks.

Mr. Draux is paid by the French government. They support traditional skills. In America, our government supports traditional skills, too. For example, my aunt makes leather belts. She cuts and dyes the leather. Then she sells the belts to various neighborhood stores. Sometimes she sells some at street fairs.

In my opinion, it is wonderful to support different arts and crafts. These arts make us feel happy. They show us that things in the world can be beautiful.

EXPLAIN YOUR SCORE

Your score? _____ Explain why you gave that score: _____

_____

STUDENT RESPONSE B:

Mr. Draux works at Versailles Palace to watch over its collection of antique clocks. He is paid by the French government. I think that it is a great idea to have someone at this job because it supports traditional skills.

EXPLAIN YOUR SCORE

Your score? _____ Explain why you gave that score: _____

_____

_____

STUDENT RESPONSE C:

Mr. Draux is the official timekeeper of the Versailles Palace in France. His job is to go around the many rooms of the palace and check the accuracy of its almost 100 antique clocks. Each clock is unique, so Mr. Draux must take it apart to see how it works before he can repair it. Because of the uniqueness of each clock, there are never instructions on how to put it together.

Mr. Draux's work shows the great importance the French place on traditional crafts. The French government provides work to thousands of craftsmen like Draux. Without such support, many people in France believe these traditional skills would be lost. Based on what their government spends and the number of people it employs for these tasks, the French have great respect for their rich past.

The support the French government provides to its traditional arts is very important. In an age when most things are mass produced, the world would drown in a sea of sameness without such crafts. These arts are not just beautiful, they also remind us of our history.

EXPLAIN YOUR SCORE

Your score? _____ Explain why you gave that score: _____

_____

_____

THE ELEMENTS OF GOOD WRITING

On the actual test, your extended response will receive a score based on five characteristics:

MEANING: How well you understand, interpret, and analyze the passage	**ORGANIZATION:** How clearly you organize your answer	**DEVELOPMENT:** How well you support your ideas with details

LANGUAGE USE: How well you express yourself	**CONVENTIONS:** How well you follow the rules of capitalization, spelling, punctuation and usage

Think of these five characteristics — *meaning*, *organization*, *development*, *language use*, and *conventions* — as the elements of good writing.

MEANING

Your extended response should show how well you *understand* the listening or reading passage and how well you can *interpret* or *analyze* it. Your response should explain what some or all of the information in the passage **means**. Often the question will have several related parts. The question on page 141 asks about Mr. Draux's work at Versailles, how this shows French support for traditional skills, and for your opinion about this. Your answer should address each part of the question.

Remember that the writing part of the test is also examining your listening or reading comprehension. Therefore, your task is two-fold: **(1)** to understand the passage; and **(2)** to use information from it to answer the question. To accomplish this, start by making sure your response answers **each** part of the question:

★ **What.** If the question asks *what*, make sure your answer identifies and describes *what* the question asks for. Here you have to *identify* *what* Draux does.

★ **How.** If the question asks *how*, be sure your answer explains or describes *how* something happens, *how* two things are alike or differ, or *how* a person changes. Here, you have to show *how* the French support traditional skills.

★ **Why.** If the question asks *why*, make sure you give the reasons *why* the event you are trying to explain happened.

★ **Give Your Opinion.** Some extended-response questions will ask you to give your own opinion or to evaluate something. Here, you have to give your opinion on French support for traditional skills. To answer this kind of question, state your opinion and the reasons behind it. Be sure to use details and examples from the listening or reading passage to support your reasons.

Now let's look at the student responses you just scored.

RESPONSE A shows some understanding of the passage. The student describes what Mr. Draux does at Versailles, and also explains that he is supported by the French government. The student then tries to make some connections beyond the text by describing an aunt. However, the student fails to make this connection clear and adds unnecessary details about the aunt. Although the student clearly expresses an opinion, the opinion fails to focus on whether the support given to traditional crafts in France is a good thing.

RESPONSE B is incomplete. Although brief, the answer does address each part of the question. However, this answer falls short in only demonstrating a very basic understanding of the passage. There is a lack of details drawn from the text, and there is no interpretation or analysis of the text.

RESPONSE C shows the best understanding of both the question and the listening passage. The student uses information from the passage to describe Mr. Draux's work at Versailles, to show how this demonstrates French support of traditional crafts, and to explain why the student thinks this is a good thing.

ORGANIZATION

Organization refers to how well you bring your ideas and details together, and the order in which your present them. Good writing has to be organized in a logical and orderly way. If not, the reader will quickly become confused. No matter how you organize your response, there are certain guidelines that all good writers use.

★ **Focus on the Task.** Make sure you keep your writing **focused**. You can achieve this by organizing your response around the requirements of the task. Usually there will be several related questions for you to answer. You might wish to answer each part of the task in a separate paragraph.

★ **A Unifying Theme.** Remember that all the different parts of the question will usually have some *common theme* or *subject matter*. In the sample question, the unifying theme is how Mr. Draux's job illustrates French support for traditional arts. Use the theme of the question to help unify your response. You may want to introduce the common theme at the beginning of your response. Then address each part of the question in a separate paragraph. Avoid including information that is unrelated to the common theme or to one of the specific question parts.

★ **Logical Flow.** There should be a logical flow or sequence of ideas in your response. This "flow" could be *chronological* (*a series of events described in the order they occur*), *cause and effect*, or *order of importance*.

★ **Transitions.** Transitions are words and phrases that show relationships or links between ideas or details. They help make your ideas and supporting details clearer to the reader. Transitions act as signposts to show the reader that you are moving from one point to the next. Some of the most common transitions include *next, then, afterwards, meanwhile, however, in addition,* and *therefore*. See page 200 for more help with transitions.

> **RESPONSE A** appears to be well organized. The first paragraph tells about Mr. Draux's work. The second discusses French support of craftsmen like Mr. Draux. However, the response goes outside the focus of the question by giving too many details about the writer's aunt.
>
> **RESPONSE B** has a unifying theme, but it lacks sufficient details for the student to organize.
>
> **RESPONSE C** has the best plan of organization. The student has chosen to discuss a separate part of the question in each paragraph. The answer addresses each part of the question, and the flow from one part to the next is smooth and logical.

DEVELOPMENT

Good writers use details and examples to explain and clarify their ideas. A good extended response gives examples and details from the listening or reading passage to illustrate its main points. These details often tell about the *who*, *what*, *when*, *where*, *how* and *why* of what the writer is describing or explaining. When writing a response, be sure to include include details from the passage to support each point you make. Be as specific as you can. The reader should be able to picture in his or her own mind the same thoughts you are trying to express.

Now look again at the three responses at the beginning of this chapter. How well are they supported with details from the listening passage?

RESPONSE A: In this response, the first paragraph is well supported with details from the passage. The student describes the work Draux performs. He is in charge of antique clocks. He goes from room to room to check their time and repair them. The second paragraph is not as well supported. It fails to provide any additional details about how the French government supports traditional skills. Instead, the student describes an aunt in America who uses traditional skills. The third paragraph has no support from the passage.

How well do the other two students support their answers?

RESPONSE B: _____

_____

RESPONSE C: _____

_____

LANGUAGE USE

Not everyone wears the same style blue jeans. People wear different styles to express themselves. Just as with clothing, there are different styles in writing. You can show your originality and creativity by the way you use language to present your ideas. Think about your readers and the impression you want to make on them. Your use of language includes your *choice of words*, *imagery*, and *sentence patterns*.

★ **Word Choice.** Interesting words help the reader to form a mental picture of what you're writing about. They help readers to *see*, *hear*, *taste*, *smell*, or *feel* what you are describing. Choose the most descriptive words you can. Avoid vague language by using specific, descriptive words. For example, "splintered" is a more precise word than "broken" because it tells readers something has broken into many pieces — too many to be repaired. A "shiny red van" is more precise and descriptive than simply writing a "car." A precise description with colorful adjectives, active verbs, and proper nouns makes it easier to picture what you are trying to express.

★ **Imagery.** You can create vivid images with *metaphors* and *similes*.

★ **Sentence Patterns.** Just as good writers consider their choice of words carefully, they also think about and vary their sentence patterns.

Which of the student responses in this chapter was the most interesting to read? Which responses had sentences with their own unique style and flavor?

RESPONSE A is clear but does not make use of many colorful or unusual words. Most of its sentence structures are short and simple.

RESPONSE B is so short that it gives its author little chance to display any individual style. Its sentences are simple and the choice of words is limited.

RESPONSE C is well written. It uses effective transitions and creates interesting images, such as "the world would drown in a sea of sameness." In addition, it contains varied sentence patterns.

CONVENTIONS

Writing conventions are the rules of standard written English — *spelling*, *capitalization*, *punctuation*, and *usage*. Your extended response will receive a separate score for how well it follows these rules. Some of the most important rules you should follow in writing your response are found in the ***Appendix*** on pages 193 to 200.

Now that you have looked at *meaning*, *organization*, *development*, *language use*, and *conventions*, what score do you think each of the responses should receive? Response C demonstrates a good understanding of the passage, has a clear focus, and completely answers the question. It is well organized and supports the points it makes with details from the passage. It uses effective transitions and vivid images without mistakes in conventions. It is clearly the best of the three responses.

THE WRITING PROCESS

You may be familiar with the ingredients of a good answer, but how should you put them all together? In this section, you will learn the four steps for drafting an answer to an extended-response question. These are sometimes known as the **steps of the writing process**:

Analyze the question	Plan your answer	Write your answer	Revise your answer

STEP 1: ANALYZE THE QUESTION

The first step in answering an extended-response question is to read the question carefully. Like a short-response question, it will ask about the listening or reading passage.

As you know, most extended-response questions will include one or more "question" words — *what*, *how*, or *why*. Extended-response questions may also ask for your *opinion*.

The key to writing your answer is to do what the "question" word asks you to do in each part of the question. Each question word should provide the *focus* for one part of your answer. In addition, the different parts of the question should be related. When you analyze the question, look for the *theme* that links its parts together.

If the question asks you to give your *opinion*, such as whether French support of traditional crafts is worthwhile, consider the arguments on both sides of the issue. Then decide your opinion and use details from the passage to support it.

STEP 2: PLAN YOUR ANSWER

After you analyze the question, you need to plan your answer. Look over your notes or the text to review the passage and to develop your own ideas to answer the question. You might wish to write down letters (**A — B — C —D**) as a quick method to refer to each bullet in the question. For example, "A" might correspond to the first part of the question — "what Mr. Draux does at Versailles." Then, jot down in note form those ideas and details you think you need to answer each part of the question. Also think how you might organize this information for your answer. You might want to start by identifying the general theme of the question. Then plan to write from one sentence to one paragraph addressing each part of the question. Generally you can answer the different parts of the question in the same order they appear in the task.

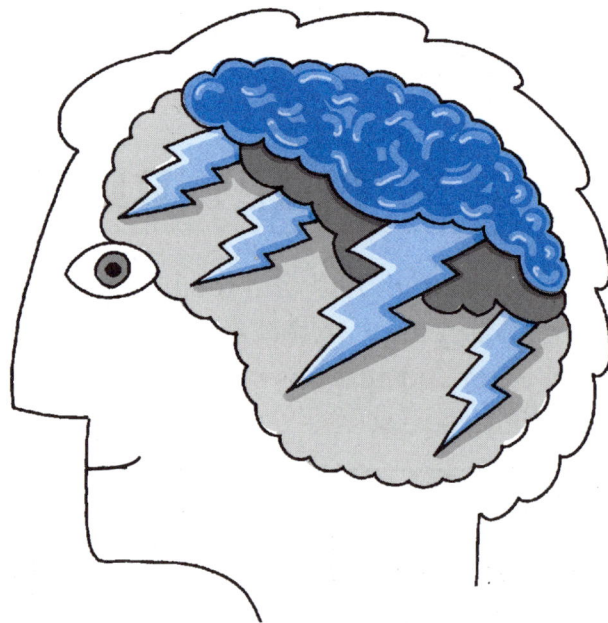

STEP 3: WRITE YOUR ANSWER

Now you are ready to write your answer. Turn each point of your plan into one or more complete sentences. Your first sentence can often *echo* the question by turning part of it into a statement. Then give your main points and supporting details. Finally, you can return to your opening idea in your conclusion. Be aware of your use of language. Make sure to use transitions between different parts of your answer. Choose precise words, vary your sentence patterns, and follow standard writing conventions.

STEP 4: REVISE YOUR ANSWER

In the final step of the writing process, read your response silently to yourself. Pretend you are someone else reading the draft for the very first time. Make sure you have answered all the parts of the question and provided examples and details from the passage to support each part of your answer.

Finally, remember that you will receive a **second score** based on your ability to follow the rules of standard written English. As you read your work, look for writing errors. Pay close attention to capitalization, punctuation, spelling, and usage. If you find something that needs to be changed, either erase it or cross it out neatly. Write insertions above the line with a "caret" mark (∧) to show where they go.

PRACTICE EXERCISE

Now you try it. Answer the following extended-response question based on the same listening passage, "Keeping Time in a Timeless Place."

According to the article, clocks were an important part of palace life. Write an essay in which you explain how the clocks at Versailles differ from clocks we have today, why they were important 300 years ago, and whether these clocks are important to preserve today. Use details from the article to support your answer.

In your answer be sure to include

- how the clocks at Versailles differ from modern ones
- why these clocks were important to palace life 300 years ago
- whether you think these clocks are important to preserve today
- details from the article to explain your opinion

Check your writing for correct spelling, grammar, and punctuation.

Write your answer to this question on a separate sheet of paper.

CHAPTER 14

A PRACTICE SESSION 2

In the last three chapters, you learned how to listen, take notes, and answer questions. In this chapter, you will listen to an informational passage similar to one on the real test. This article is called, "What Killed the Dinosaurs," and is found in the *Teacher's Guide and Answer Key* that accompanies this book. Your teacher will read the article two times. As you listen each time, you can take notes on a separate sheet of paper. Then answer the questions that follow.

1 Complete the chart below by describing three effects of the large meteorite that struck the Earth 65 million years ago. Use details from the article to support your answer.

Effects of Giant Meteorite Crash	
1	
2	
3	

2 Using details from the article, describe the Deccan Traps.

3   Explain how some mammals were able to survive the disasters discussed in the article. Use details from the article to support your answer.

4   The author of "What Killed the Dinosaurs?" writes that many scientists think a large meteorite crash together with a series of lava flows ended the age of the dinosaurs. Write an essay in which you explain your opinion as to which of these two events was more important in killing off the dinosaurs. Use details from the article to support your answer.

In your response be sure to

- explain how the meteorite crash helped kill the dinosaurs
- explain how the lava flows also contributed to killing the dinosaurs
- give your opinion of which event was more important
- use details from the article to support your opinion

Check your writing for correct spelling, grammar, and punctuation.

Write your answer to this question on a separate sheet of paper.

SESSION 3:
READING AND WRITING

In **Session 3**, you will read two passages that are related in some way. Then you will be asked to answer one extended-response and three short-response questions about them.

You already know how to answer both short-response and extended-response questions from **Session 2**. In **Session 3**, you will have the ability to look over the passages to help you write your answers. Some of the questions will ask you to make connections between both reading passages.

In **Chapter 15**, you will learn how to approach paired readings. This is followed by a complete practice **Session 3** in **Chapter 16**.

ANALYZING PAIRED READINGS

In **Session 3** you will be asked to read two passages. After reading the passages, you will be asked to answer **one** extended-response and **three** short-response questions. Most or all of the short-response questions will focus on one of the two readings. The extended-response question will usually ask about **both** readings. In this chapter, you will learn how to answer questions about paired readings.

WHAT ARE PAIRED READINGS?

One of the reading passages in **Session 3** will be a literary text, such as a story or poem. The other passage will be an informational text. The two passages will be *related* or *linked* in some way.

★ **Subject.** The two passages may deal with the same *subject*. Information in one reading may help to explain what happens in the other reading. For example, both passages might examine the challenges of urban life. The first passage could be a report about growing up in a large modern city. The second could be a story about a young girl's experiences at school.

★ **Theme.** The two passages may deal with the same *theme*. For example, both texts might focus on feelings of anger or acts of courage.

As you read the passages, remember to use the strategies of good readers:

Ask Yourself Questions	Make Mental Pictures	Make Predictions	Make Connections

Think about What is Important	Summarize	Solve Problems

Also ask yourself these special questions when reading linked passages:

★ **What type of reading is each passage?**

★ **What are some of the main ideas or themes of each reading?**

★ **What do the two readings have in common?**

★ **How do the two readings differ?**

SAMPLE LINKED PASSAGES

Now that you know how to approach linked passages, read the following two selections. These passages are similar to those you might find on the actual test.

THE STORY OF SCARFACE

There once lived among a tribe of Indians a poor boy whose father and mother were dead, and who had no friends. The boy grew up strong and brave. While he was young, he met a grizzly bear, which he fought and killed. During the struggle the bear set its claws in the boy's face and tore it cruelly; when the wound healed it left an unsightly red mark, so he became known as Scarface.

The boy thought little of his disfigurement until he fell in love with the beautiful daughter of the chief of his tribe. When he saw all the young braves in splendid dress paying court to this maiden, his heart ached sorely because he was poor, friendless, and above all bore a terrible disfiguring scar. But the maiden did not care for the finery of the young Indians who asked for her hand in marriage. Scarface scarcely dared to approach her, but the girl often saw him as he went about the forest. She felt he was braver and truer than all of the other braves.

One day, Scarface passed by and looked at her, showing the love and admiration that possessed him. He drew nearer to her, knowing that if he did not speak at once his courage would leave him. "Maiden," he said, "I am poor and my face is unsightly to look at. But my heart is full of love for you, and I would greatly desire you to be my wife."

The girl looked at him and saw the love in his face. "That you are poor," she said, "matters little. But I may not be the bride of any man. The great Lord of the Sun has forbidden me to marry." Scarface's heart sank at these words. Yet he refused to give up hope. "Will the Lord of the Sun not release you?"

CONTINUED ➤

"Go to him." said the maiden. "Ask if he will free me from my promise. And that I may know that he has done so, ask him to take the scar off your face as a sign."

"I will seek out the god in his land, and beg him to pity us," said Scarface.

He turned and set off on his journey. He traveled for many miles. Through forests and over mountains he went, searching for the gates that marked the entrance to the country of the great god. Day after day he journeyed until he was weary, taking but short rests.

Each morning he hoped that evening would bring him to the gates. But after a long period of travel, it seemed that his labor and weariness had been for nothing. He came to a river that he could not cross. He felt all hope dying in his heart. But then he saw two beautiful swans. "We will take you across the water," they said. They glided across to the opposite shore, carrying Scarface on their backs.

"Go along the road that lies before you, and you will come to the golden gates," the swans told Scarface. He had not gone far when he saw lying on the ground a very beautiful bow and arrows. He thought they must belong to a mighty hunter. Much as he wanted to take them, he walked on because he was honest.

Soon a young man came upon him and said, "I have lost my bow and arrows along this road. Have you seen them?" Scarface directed the youth to the bow and arrows he had seen on the road. When the youth returned, he asked Scarface where he was going. "I seek the great Lord of the Sun," replied Scarface. The youth smiled, "I am Morning Star and the Sun is my father. I will take you to him."

The two went down the road and passed through the gates. Scarface was bewildered by the beauty of everything around him. Moon Goddess cared for him, and he soon felt refreshed and strong.

CONTINUED ▶

After awhile the Lord of the Sun visited him. "Stay with us," he said. "You are weary, and have traveled a long way to see me. Be my guest for a season." Happily, Scarface replied, "I will stay, Great Lord."

Each morning Scarface and Morning Star went hunting and returned at night. The Lord of the Sun warned them, "Never go near the Great Water, for savage birds dwell there that seek to slay my son Morning Star."

Despite this warning, Morning Star longed to meet these birds and kill them. One day he stole away from Scarface and traveled to the water. Scarface, suddenly realizing that Morning Star was gone, hurried off toward the dreaded birds. Soon, he heard horrid cries. He rushed to the birds around Morning Star, taking them by surprise, so that they flew off. Then he carried Morning Star to safety.

When they returned to the lodge, the Lord of the Sun told Scarface, "You have saved my son. How may I repay you?" Scarface took courage and replied, "There is a maiden whom I love. She is the daughter of the chief. I am a poor warrior and hideous to look at. Yet I know she would marry me, but for the respect she holds for your commands. She has promised you, Great Lord, that she will marry no man."

Then the Sun God spoke: "Go back and take this maiden for your wife. Tell her that it is my will that she marry you." The God then passed his hand over the Indian's face, and immediately the disfiguring scar vanished. "Tell her to look and she will see how the Lord of the Sun has restored your face."

Then the Lord of the Sun and Morning Star loaded him with gifts and changed his poor clothes for the rich dress of an Indian chef. Scarface no longer, he traveled quickly and was soon home once more.

The chief's daughter failed to recognize him when she first saw him. A second look told her who he was. Realizing the scar was gone, and remembering what its disappearance meant, she ran to him with a cry of joy. The story of his journey was told and the chief gladly gave his daughter to this warrior on whom the Sun God had looked with favor. That same day they were married, and the chief gave his daughter a splendid wigwam as a wedding present.

MY JOURNEY BACK TO LIFE

by Lance Armstrong

Lance Armstrong was a successful athlete when he was struck with cancer. He survived his treatment, built up his body again, and went on to the win the *Tour de France* — the world's most famous bicycle race. In this excerpt from his autobiography, Armstrong tells about his feelings in overcoming cancer.

I'm asking you to put aside your ideas about heroes and miracles because I'm not storybook material. I'll give you an example. I've read that I flew up the hills and mountains of France. But you don't fly up a hill. You struggle slowly and painfully up a hill, and maybe, if you work very hard, you get to the top ahead of everybody else.

Cancer is like that, too. Good, strong people get cancer, and they do all the right things to beat it, and they still die. That is the essential truth you learn. People die. And after you learn it, all other matters seem unimportant and small.

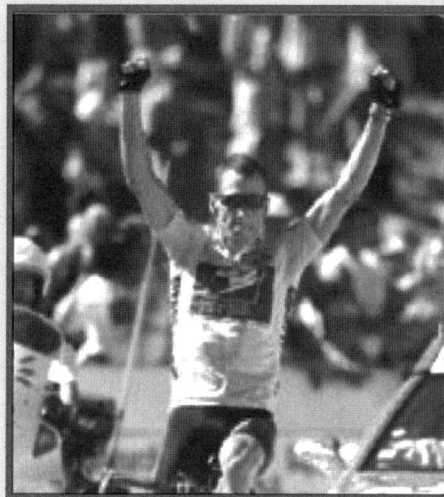

Lance Armstrong

I don't know why I'm still alive. I have a strong body, and my profession taught me how to compete against long odds and big obstacles. I like to train hard and race hard. That helped. It was a good start, but it wasn't the determining factor. I can't help feeling my survival was a matter of blind luck.

Basically, I can endure more physical stress than most people can, and I don't get as tired when I'm doing it. So I figure maybe that helped me live. I was lucky — I was born with above-average capacity for breathing. But even so, I was in a desperate, sick fog much of the time when I was ill.

My illness was humbling and revealing. It forced me to look over my life with an unforgiving eye. There are some shameful episodes in it: instances of meanness, unfinished tasks, weakness, and regrets. I had to ask myself, "If I live, who do I intend to be?" I found I had a lot of answering to do as a man.

Everybody's favorite question is "How did cancer change you?" The real question is: how didn't it change me? I left my house on October 2, 1996, as one person and came home another.

CONTINUED

I was a world-class athlete. I was one of the top riders in the world. I returned a different person literally. Even my body is different, because during the chemotherapy* I lost all the muscle I had ever built up. When I recovered it didn't come back in the same way.

The truth is that cancer was the best thing that ever happened to me. I don't know why I got the illness, but it did wonders for me, and I wouldn't want to walk away from it. Why would I want to change the most important and shaping event in my life?

Lance Armstrong racing on his bike

People die. Why should we go on, you might ask? But there is another truth, too. People live. It's an equal and opposing truth. When I was sick, I saw more beauty and triumph and truth in a single day than I ever did in a bike race — but they were human movements, not miraculous ones. I met a guy in a fraying sweatshirt who turned out to be a brilliant surgeon. I became friends with a hard-working and overscheduled nurse, who gave me such great care. I saw children with no eyelashes or eyebrows who lost their hair from chemo, who fought with the hearts of world-class athletes. I still don't completely understand it.

---

* **chemotherapy.** The use of drugs to kill cancer cells. Often patients receiving chemotherapy feel very sick during treatment.

COMPARING PAIRED PASSAGES

Now that you have read *The Story of Scarface* and *My Journey Back to Life*, let's look at four questions you should think about when reading linked passages.

WHAT TYPE OF READING IS EACH PASSAGE?

THE STORY OF SCARFACE **Literary: Tribal Legend**	*MY JOURNEY BACK TO LIFE* **Informational: Personal Essay**

WHAT ARE THE MAIN IDEAS OR THEMES OF EACH READING?

THE STORY OF SCARFACE

This is the legend of an Indian brave who is poor and without parents or friends. He goes through life with an ugly scar on his face. It is a tale of hardship, patience and determination. Scarface falls in love with the chief's daughter, who sees a brave, strong warrior behind his poverty and disfiguring scar. But she cannot marry him, or anyone else, until she is granted permission by the Sun God. To win her love, Scarface must journey to the Sun God and ask him to change his command. After many days, Scarface reaches the land of the Sun God. After Scarface saves Morning Star, he asks the Sun God for permission to marry the chief's daughter. The god gives his permission and removes the ugly scar from his face.

MY JOURNEY BACK TO LIFE

This excerpt is a personal essay by Lance Armstrong, winner of the *Tour de France*. Besides being a world-class athlete, Armstrong has struggled against cancer. His essay tells about his experiences and feelings both as an athlete and as a cancer patient. While his strength and determination helped him to survive, Armstrong thinks it was also a matter of luck.

WHAT DO THE TWO PASSAGES HAVE IN COMMON?

Both passages deal with the subject of meeting challenges. Scarface goes on a journey to reach the Sun God. Lance Armstrong also experiences a journey, to survive cancer and resume his career as a world-class athlete. Both Scarface and Armstrong show strength and determination in their journeys, and both benefit from "blind luck."

HOW DO THE TWO READINGS DIFFER?

The two readings differ in important ways. *The Story of Scarface* is a Native American legend. Although Native Americans believed it was true, it has a make-believe setting, characters, and plot. *My Journey Back to Life* is an informational text about real events. It describes the author's actual thoughts about his battle with cancer.

SHORT-RESPONSE QUESTIONS

Now that you have analyzed and compared these linked passages, you are ready to tackle the kinds of questions that might appear on the test. Answer the three short-response questions below. They are similar to the questions you will find on **Session 3** of the actual test. Remember, you can look over the readings to help you answer each question.

1 **In the boxes below, list three things that Scarface did in order to marry the chief's daughter.**

1.	2.	3.

2 **Describe how Scarface helped Morning Star, the son of the Lord of the Sun. Use details from the story to support your answer.**

3 **In *My Journey Back to Life*, Lance Armstrong writes, "I can't help feeling my survival was more a matter of blind luck." Using information from the essay, explain what he means.**

To answer these questions, take the same steps that you used for answering short-response questions in Chapter 12 (*see page 130*).

STRATEGIES FOR SUCCESS

First, look at the question carefully. Pay special attention to any "question words" — **what**, **why**, or **how**. Remember that before you start to answer the question, you must be sure to understand what it asks for.

Next, see if you can answer the question based on what you remember about the passage. Then look over one or both passages to check what you have recalled and to find additional details. As you scan the text, make a checkmark in the margin wherever you find relevant information. These checkmarks will help you to locate this information as you write your answer.

Finally, write your answer clearly and neatly. Be sure you answer the question. After you write your answer, ask yourself:
Is my answer based on supporting details found one or both reading passages?

EXTENDED-RESPONSE QUESTIONS

The extended-response question in **Session 3** will usually require you to use information from both readings. This is where you will need to draw connections between the two passages. Examine the sample question below:

4

Scarface and Lance Armstrong both faced challenges that seemed impossible to overcome. Write an essay in which you describe the qualities each possessed and how these qualities helped them to meet the challenges they faced. Be sure to use information from both passages in your answer.

In your answer, be sure to include

- a description of the challenges each faced
- the qualities they possessed
- an explanation of how these qualities helped them meet the challenges
- details from both passages to support your answer

Check your writing for correct spelling, grammar, and punctuation.

To answer this question, take the same steps you learned in Chapter 13 for answering other extended-response questions. Let's briefly review those steps:

★ **Step 1. Analyze the Question.** First, read the question carefully. Look at the question as a whole and make sure you understand exactly what the question asks for. The question on the previous page focuses on the characteristics that helped both Scarface and Armstrong succeed. Next, look at the parts of the question. One part is a "**what**" question: *what* are the qualities of the characters. The next part is a "**how**" question: *how* did the qualities help?

★ **Step 2. Plan Your Answer.** Think about the two passages and what you should write. Then scan the two reading passages for additional helpful information. Place a checkmark in the margin wherever the text shows how the characters' qualities helped them. This will provide you with the supporting details you will need for your response.

Based on the information you gather from both passages, it may help to create a short list of points you can refer to as you answer the question:

	Quality	**How it Helped**
Scarface		
Lance Armstrong		

Once you have listed all your ideas and supporting details, you have to organize them to write your response. You should organize them into some form of prewriting plan. Include an **introduction** that states the focus of your essay, which should be based on the question. For the **body of your essay**, write down your points and supporting details in some logical order. For example, you might organize details in *time order*.

★ **Step 3. Write Your Answer.** Now simply turn your plan into your written answer. Make sure you use information from **both** passages in your response. Use colorful and precise words, including energetic, active verbs. Avoid vague or confusing sentences. Keep your writing natural. Do not try to impress the reader with words you are not sure how to use.

★ **Step 4. Revise Your Answer.** Read over your response before you hand it in. Make sure that your response stays focused on answering the question. Be sure you have included all of your best ideas. Add anything you may have left out, and take out whatever you feel does not belong. As you revise your answer, the key question you must ask yourself is:

> *Have I really explained how the qualities of Scarface and Lance Armstrong helped them to meet the challenges they faced?*

Give your final response a neat appearance that is easy to read. Keep a margin on both sides of the paper. Begin each paragraph on a new line. Indent each new paragraph. Finally, check your writing for errors in punctuation, spelling, capitalization and usage. Remember that you will receive a separate score for how well you follow standard writing conventions.

PRACTICE EXERCISE

In this chapter, you have learned how to write an answer to an extended-response question for **Session 3**. Now it's your turn. Try answering the following question using the linked passages you read earlier in this chapter.

> In *My Journey Back to Life*, Lance Armstrong writes "I can't help feeling my survival was more a matter of blind luck." Were the successes of Lance Armstrong and Scarface in overcoming obstacles more a matter of determination or of luck? Write an essay in which you explain your opinion. Use details from **both** passages to support your answer.
>
> In your answer, be sure to include
>
> • how Scarface overcame obstacles
> • how Lance Armstrong overcame obstacles
> • whether determination or luck was more important in each case
> • details from both the story and the excerpt to support your answer

Check your writing for correct spelling, grammar, and punctuation.

CHAPTER 16

A PRACTICE SESSION 3

In this chapter, you will practice your new skills by answering three short-response questions and one extended-response question based on two linked passages — just as you will on **Session 3** of the actual test.

THE BELL OF ATRI

Retold by James Baldwin (1841–1925)

Atri is the name of a very old town in Italy built halfway up the side of a steep hill. Long ago, the king of the region bought a fine large bell and had it hung up in a tower in the marketplace. A long rope that reached almost to the ground was fastened to the bell. The smallest child could ring the bell by pulling upon this rope.

"It is the bell of justice," said the king.

When at last everything was ready, the people of Atri came down to the marketplace to look at the bell of justice. It was a pretty bell and was polished until it looked almost as bright and yellow as the sun.

"How we should like to hear it ring!" they said. Then the king came down the street. And everybody stood very still and waited to see if he would ring it.

But he did not ring the bell. When he came to the tower, he stopped and raised his hand. "My people," he said, "do you see this bell? It is your bell. But it must never be rung except in case of need. If one of you is wronged at any time, come and ring the bell. And then the judges shall come together at once, and hear your case, and give you justice. Rich and poor, old and young, all alike may come. But no one must touch the rope unless you know that you have been wronged."

CONTINUED ➡

Many years passed by. Many times the bell in the marketplace rang out to call the judges together. Many wrongs were righted, many ill-doers were punished. At last the rope was almost worn out. Some strands were broken; it became so short only someone tall could reach it.

"This will never do," said the judges one day. "What if a child should be wronged? The child could not ring the bell to let us know it." They gave orders that a new rope should be put upon the bell so that the smallest child could reach it. But there was no rope to be found in all of Atri. They would have to send across the mountains, and it would be many days to bring it. What if some great wrong should be done before it came? How would the judges know about it, if the injured one couldn't reach the old rope?

"Let me fix it for you," said a man who stood by. He ran to his garden, and soon came back with a long grapevine in his hands. "This will do for a rope," he said. And he climbed up and fastened it to the bell. The slender vine, with its leaves and long curled tendrils, reached to the ground.

"Yes," said the judges, "it is a very good rope. Let it be as it is."

Now, on the hillside above the village, there lived a man who in his youth had once been a brave knight. He had traveled through many lands and fought many battles. His best friend through all that time had been his horse — a strong, noble steed that had borne him safely through many a danger. But the knight, as he grew older, cared no more to ride into battle; he thought of nothing but gold; he became a miser. He sold all he had, and went to live in a hut on the hillside. Day after day he sat among his money bags and planned how he might get more gold. And day after day his horse stood in his bare stall, hungry and shivering with cold.

"What is the use of keeping that lazy steed?" said the miser one morning. "It costs me more to keep him than he's worth. I might sell him, but there is no one who wants him. I'll let him go to shift for himself and pick grass by the roadside." So the old horse was sent out to find what he could on the barren hillside.

Lame and sick, he strolled the dusty roads, glad to find a blade of grass to eat. One afternoon, the horse wandered into the marketplace. Not a man nor child was there, for the heat of the sun had driven them indoors.

The gates were wide open; the poor beast then saw the grapevine rope that hung from the bell of justice. The leaves and tendrils upon it were fresh and green. He stretched his neck and took one of the tempting morsels in his mouth. It was hard to break it from the vine.

CONTINUED ▶

He pulled at it, and the bell above began to ring. All the people in Atri heard it. It seemed to say,

Someone   has done   me wrong!
Oh! come   and judge   my case!
For I've   been wronged!

The judges heard it. They put on their robes and went to the marketplace. They wondered who rang the bell. As they passed through the gate, they saw the old horse nibbling the vine. "Ha!" cried one, "It's the miser's steed. He has come to call for justice. His master, as everyone knows, has treated him shamefully."

"He pleads his cause as well as any animal can," said another. "And he shall have justice!" said the third. Meanwhile a crowd had come to the marketplace to learn of the case the judges were about to try. When they saw the horse, all stood still in wonder. Everyone was ready to tell how they'd seen him wandering on the hills, unfed, uncared for, while his master sat at home counting his gold.

"Bring the miser before us," said the judges. When he came, they made him hear their judgment. "This horse has served you for many years and saved you from many a danger. We order that half your gold be set aside to buy him shelter, food, a pasture for him to graze on, and a warm stall to comfort him in his old age."

The miser hung his head, saddened to lose his gold. But the people shouted with joy, and the horse was led away to his new stall and a dinner such as he had not eaten in many a day.

1 **What effect does the king's bell have on the villagers of Atri? Use details from the story to support your answer**

2 Using details from the story, complete the chart below.

	What He Cares About	How He Treats His Horse
The knight in his youth		
The knight living on the hillside above Atri		

FROM JUSTICE TO DEMOCRACY BY WAY OF THE BELLS

This speech was given by José Saramago of Portugal, winner of the 1998 Nobel Prize for Literature.

I will begin by telling you about a notable episode in peasant life that took place four hundred years ago in a village near Florence, Italy. People were sitting in their houses or working in the fields, busy with their own affairs, when suddenly the church bell was heard to ring. Those were more religious times — we are talking about the 16th Century — and the bells often rang several times a day, so there should have been nothing to wonder about. But this bell was ringing in a slow rhythm as if for the dead, and that was surprising, because no one from the village was known to be dying.

José Saramago of Portugal

CONTINUED →

So the women rounded up their children, the men left their work in the fields, and soon all gathered in front of the church, waiting to be told whom they should mourn. The bell went on ringing for a few more minutes and finally fell silent. Moments later the door opened and a solitary peasant appeared.

Now, as this was not the man who normally rang the bell, his neighbors understandably asked him where the bell-ringer was and who had died. "The bell-ringer's not here and it was me who rang the bell," the peasant answered. "Then no one's dead?" his neighbors asked. To which the peasant responded: "No one with the name of a person. I rang the bell for *justice* because justice is dead."

For some time, he explained, a greedy lord had been moving the boundary stones, invading the peasant's own small plot, which shrank with each advance. The peasant had protested and complained, then begged for mercy, and finally complained to the authorities to seek justice. All in vain: the stealing continued. In desperation, he decided to announce to the world that justice was dead. Perhaps he thought his gesture would stir all the bells in the world and set them ringing: that all of them would join in ringing and not be silenced until justice was brought back to life. Such a clamor, flying from village to village, leaping borders, surely would awaken the sleeping world...

I do not know what happened next, whether the townspeople went to help the peasant move back the boundary markers or whether his neighbors, now that justice was declared to be dead, hung their heads in resignation, and went back to their daily sad existence.

I guess that this was the only time in the world that a bell, after so often tolling the death of human beings, sadly rang for the death of justice itself. The funeral chant of the village was never heard again, but justice continues to die. At this very moment, both far away and nearby, someone is killing it.

Each time justice dies, it is as if it had never existed for those who trusted in it, for those who had expected what we all have the right to expect: simply justice. We have the right to a modest justice, a justice as necessary to the happiness of the spirit as food for the body is necessary for life. This should be the justice practiced in the courts, but first and foremost it should be a form of justice coming spontaneously from society itself. We have a right to justice that is as evident as an inescapable moral command, the respect for the rights of every human person.

3 **Why did the Florentine peasant feel that justice was dead? Use details from the speech to support your answer.**

EXTENDED-RESPONSE QUESTION

4 José Saramago argues that each of us has the right to expect some degree of justice. Write an essay in which you explain your opinion of what justice is and tell whether the horse in the story and the peasant in Saramago's speech received it. Be sure to use information from both passages to support your answer.

In your answer, be sure to include

- your opinion of what justice is
- an explanation of whether the horse and peasant received justice
- details from both the story and the speech to support your answer

Check your writing for correct spelling, grammar, and punctuation.

Now, use a separate sheet of paper to plan and write your answer.

CHAPTER 17

A PRACTICE GRADE 8 ENGLISH LANGUAGE ARTS TEST

Now that you have mastered **New York's Grade 8 English Language Arts Standards**, let's see how well prepared you are for the **English Language Arts Test**. Before you begin, take a moment to preview what you will find on the test:

★ The test is divided into three sessions. Today you will take **Session 1**. Tomorrow you will take **Session 2**. On the third day you will take **Session 3**.

★ **Session 1** of the test consists of five reading selections and 26 multiple-choice questions. You will have **45 minutes** to complete **Session 1**. Read each selection carefully. Think before choosing your response.

★ When you see the word **STOP** at the bottom of the page, you have finished the session. You may go back and check your work for that session only. Do not go on to the next day's session.

★ Once you finish checking your work, sit quietly and do not disturb other students.

★ You will have 45 minutes to complete **Session 2**, and 60 minutes to complete **Session 3**.

★ For **Session 2** and **Session 3**, you may print your answers or write in cursive. Be sure to write clearly and neatly.

Taking this practice **Grade 8 English Language Arts Test** will help you to identify those areas where you may still need to improve. We recommend that you take this practice test with your class under "test conditions" in a quiet room without distractions.

Good luck on this practice test!

SESSION 1

Directions: In this part of the test, you will do some reading and answer questions about what you have read. Read this article about a famous Spanish road known as *El Camino Real*. Then answer questions 1 through 6.

EL CAMINO REAL

by Robert J. Torrez

For more than two centuries, *El Camino de Tierra Adentro* — the road to the interior — was the main line of communication and trade between the Spanish government in Mexico City and the distant frontier outpost of Santa Fe in New Mexico. This road extended for more than sixteen hundred miles. Whatever the people of New Mexico needed that they could not make themselves had to be transported over this road.

Because the road belonged to the King of Spain, it also was called "*El Camino Real*," or the royal road. It followed ancient Native American trade routes.

In 1540, the Spanish government sent Francisco Vasquez de Coronado to search for the fabled Seven Cities of Gold, which were believed to exist somewhere in the vast and unexplored lands we now call North America. Coronado and his men explored much of the present-day Southwest for two years before returning to Mexico.

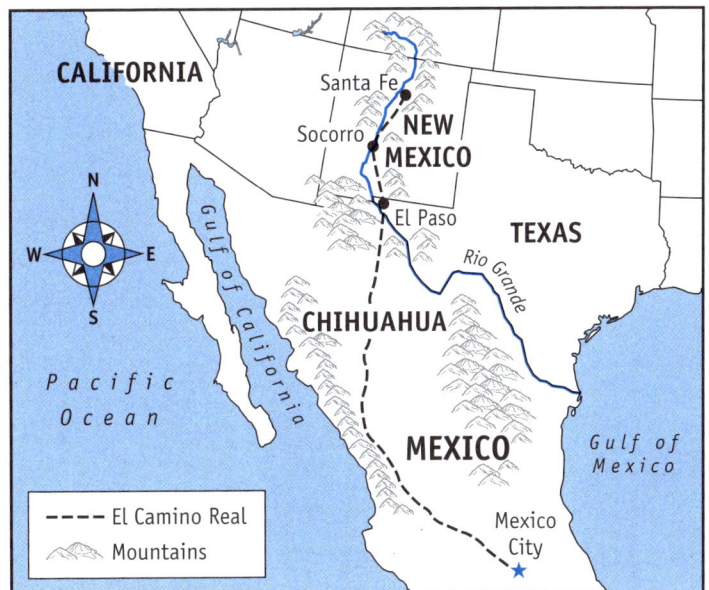

In 1581, a Spanish priest obtained permission from Spanish authorities to go north from Mexico to explore the region visited by Coronado forty years earlier. The priest and his companions disappeared without a trace after they decided to stay in the north to convert the Native Americans to Christianity.

The following year, an expedition was sent northward from Mexico along this ancient route to search for the missing priests. Although they failed to find the priests, the members of the expedition are credited with the first use of the term "*La Nueva Mexico*" to describe the region now known as New Mexico. The expedition was also the first to enter the region with wagons, opening a road along the route that eventually became *El Camino Real*. When New Mexico was colonized in 1598, the settlers followed the wagon tracks left by the expedition.

For 250 years, *El Camino Real* helped keep New Mexico in touch with the Spanish colonial government in Mexico. Every two or three years, a supply train of wagons loaded with goods headed north from Mexico to Sante Fe. Each vehicle was pulled by eight mules or oxen. The wagons carried items not produced in New Mexico, such as sugar, olive oil, and chocolate, as well as other items needed by the Spanish colonists, including paper, medicine, musical instruments, iron, and gunpowder. *El Camino Real* was vital for the colony's survival.

The supply train and its military escort set off from Chihuahua (*a Mexican province*) and headed north, traveling ten miles or so a day. After crossing northern Mexico, the caravan arrived at the Rio Grande ("Great River"). Here the wagons forded the river and continued northward along its banks, pausing to rest at various *parajes* or "stopping places," before arriving at the dreaded *Jornada del Muerto*, a hundred-mile stretch of desert extending through southern New Mexico.

At the northern end of the desert, the people of the caravan were greatly relieved when they reached the settlement of Senecu, south of present-day Socorro, New Mexico. From here, the traveling was much easier and safer, as the road entered the more heavily settled and cultivated portion of the Rio Grande valley.

Finally, six months after first leaving Mexico, the caravan would arrive in Santa Fe. Officials opened pouches with important documents. Citizens, anxious for news from home, received mail. Wagons were unloaded and their supplies distributed. For the next four to six months, goods from the missions and settlements were gathered for the return trip to Mexico. Flocks of sheep, raw wool, buffalo and deer hides, salt, wool blankets, and women's stockings were all packed into the wagons. Then the caravan began its long trip south, completing another round of trade and communication over *El Camino Real*.

---

1   What was the author's main purpose in writing this article?

   A   to show the location of *El Camino Real*

   B   to illustrate some of the products transported along *El Camino Real*

   C   to explain the importance of *El Camino Real* to New Mexico

   D   to explain how the name *El Camino Real* came into existence

2   The road was sometimes called "*El Camino Real*" because it

   F   was owned by Spanish settlers   **H**   led to the interior of Mexico

   G   belonged to the King of Spain   **J**   had been used by Aztec kings

3   Which **best** describes the path of supply trains along *El Camino Real*?

   A   from Mexico City to El Paso to Chihuahua

   B   from Chihuahua to Socorro to Sante Fe

   C   from Chihuahua to Mexico City to El Paso

   D   from Mexico City to Socorro to Chihuahua

4   Which statement best shows the importance of *El Camino Real*?

   F   "*El Camino Real* was vital for the colony's survival."

   G   "The heavily laden supply train and its military escort set off from southern Chihuahua and headed north."

   H   "Wagons were unloaded and their supplies distributed."

   J   "Each vehicle was pulled by eight mules or oxen."

5   The information in the article appears to be reliable because the author

   A   uses specific facts to support his descriptions

   B   personally witnessed the events he is writing about

   C   had ancestors who traveled on *El Camino Real*

   D   was personally engaged in trade with Mexico

6 Study the index below from a guidebook about New Mexico.

> Fairs and Festivals 45-62
>   Latin Dance Festival 49-50
>   Harvest Festival 52-53
>   Salman Ranch Raspberry Festival 60-62
> History 67-71
> Holidays 14-30
> Museums 76-81

Which pages would **most likely** offer more information about *El Camino Real*?

F pages 14–30   **H** pages 67–71

G pages 45–62   **J** pages 76–81

Directions: Read the movie poster to the right. Then answer questions 7 and 8.

7 What is the purpose of this poster?

A to inform people of the risks of war

B to stir troops to fight with courage

C to persuade people to watch this movie

D to entertain viewers with a collage

8 The message appearing across the soldier's helmet gives

F facts to help readers make an informed judgment.

G the opinion of an authority on the nature of war.

H an exaggerated statement that is unsupported by facts.

J praise to other news stories about the war.

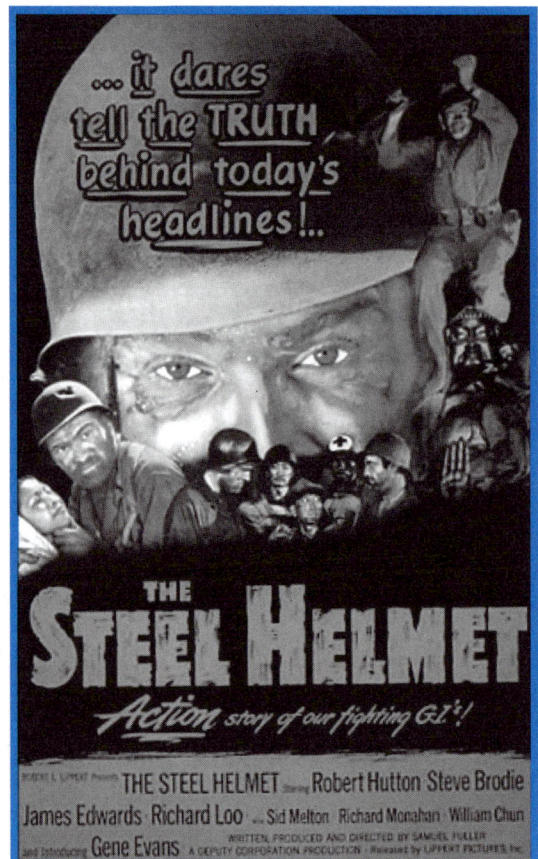

Read this folktale from East Africa. Then answer questions 9 through 14.

THE LION'S WHISKER

Once there lived a husband and wife in a village in Ethiopia. The husband was not happy with their marriage and often came home late from his work in the fields. Sometimes he failed to come home at all.

His wife loved him very much, but she was also unhappy with their relationship. She finally decided to talk to the oldest and wisest man in the village. The old man had married them years earlier and now she asked him to end their marriage.

The village elder listened patiently to her bitter words but responded with kindness. "Separation is not always best. I know of a far better way. I will prepare a secret potion that will change your husband into an obedient and loving man. He will come home on time and always try to please you."

"Prepare this medicine at once, old man!" cried the woman. For she truly wanted to stay married.

"That is not easy to do," replied the wise man. "I lack one vital ingredient to make the potion. I need a single whisker taken from a living lion. If you bring me such a whisker, I will prepare my secret potion."

"I will get it for you," she said with determination.

The following morning, the woman carried a large chunk of raw meat to the river where the lion often came to drink. Hiding behind a clump of bushes, she patiently waited quietly until the lion appeared.

CONTINUED ➤

The woman was frightened of the lion and wanted to run away, but somehow she found the courage to toss the meat to the beast. The lion quickly devoured the meat and walked slowly back to the trees. The next morning, the woman fed the lion again and every morning for the rest of the week. During the second week she crept out of hiding and let the lion see who was bringing his breakfast. In the third week, she moved closer and closer to the feeding lion.

After four weeks had passed, she was able to sit quietly next to him as he ate. Thus, it became possible one day for her to gently reach over and pluck a single whisker from the lion's chin.

She ran to the wise man with the prize and pleaded with him to make the secret potion at once! He was surprised to see the lion's whisker and demanded to know how the woman had acquired it. Upon hearing her story, the old man said, "You do not need magic to change the ways of your husband. You are brave enough to pull a whisker from a living lion. This task required cleverness, courage, and patience. If you can accomplish this, then can you not use the same cleverness, courage, and patience to improve your marriage?"

He continued: "Do not get angry with your husband. Instead, show him each day that you love him. Gently point out that you, too, want to be respected and loved. Share his problems and make him feel wanted. Give him time to change and see what will happen."

The woman went home that day and put the old man's advice to work. Slowly, the relationship with her husband began to improve. Within a year, their life together grew into one of happiness that lasted for a lifetime.

9   The central conflict of the story could **best** be described as the struggle of

    A   a woman to train a wild lion

    B   a village elder to discipline an unruly wife

    C   a woman to save her marriage

    D   a wise man to obtain a lion's whisker for a magical potion

10   Read this sentence from the story.

> **The lion quickly devoured the meat
> and walked slowly back to the trees.**

The word "devoured" means the same as

  F   refused
  G   ate up
  H   altered
  J   put away

11   The story takes place in a village whose people

  A   look to the village elder for advice
  B   use research to solve problems
  C   depend on science to explain things
  D   follow traditional church teachings

12   Why did the woman want a whisker from the chin of a lion?

  F   to show her husband how brave she was
  G   to demonstrate her daring to the people of her village
  H   to show her husband how determined she was
  J   to make a magical portion to gain her husband's love

13   What emotion did the woman **most likely** feel after receiving the old man's advice at the end of the story?

  A   amusement
  B   jealousy
  C   hope
  D   despair

14   What lesson can **best** be learned from the story?

  F   A good marriage requires patience and understanding.
  G   Never overestimate one's own powers out of vanity.
  H   Do not let your hopes carry you away from reality.
  J   Take whatever you can get when you can.

Read this essay by Anna Quindlen, a noted columnist and commentator on modern society. Then answer questions 15 through 21.

HOW READING CHANGED MY LIFE

by Anna Quindlen

As I grew up thrilled by books, I began to think that women read differently than men. Statistics, although slippery things, suggest some of those differences: a poll taken in 1991 showed that women were more likely than men to find reading a more relaxing pastime than watching television. And women are more productive readers: college-educated women reported reading an average of twenty-five books over the space of a year, while their male counterparts had read only fifteen.

Some bookstore owners say their women customers are more likely to read novels, while the men choose more biographies and history. Perhaps women feel more of a need to escape their own lives and take up those of others than men do.

But it seemed to me, listening to members of various book clubs talk about what they did and why, that, like so much else, women seem to see reading not only as a solitary activity but as an opportunity for emotional connection, not just to the characters in a novel but to those who are reading or have read the same novels themselves. We pass on beloved books to friends, discuss them on the phone.

A collision of two female cultures may have resulted in the sudden surplus of book groups: the women's movement insisted we do something, be something, use our minds as well as our hearts, while in daily life many of us were surrounded by the mundane, the sink full of dishes, car pools, screaming children. A book group provides one small way for the two selves to coexist: a carefully scheduled time for intellectual exercise mixed with female companionship.

And a book provides what it always has: a haven. I remember the first year after my second child was born, what I can remember of it at all, as a year of overturned glasses of milk, of toys on the floor, of hours from sunrise to sunset that were horribly busy but filled with what, at the end of the day, seemed like absolutely nothing at all.

What saved my sanity were books. What saved my sanity was disappearing, if only for fifteen minutes before I inevitably began to nod off in bed, into the dark and placid English rooms of Anita Brookner's newest novel, into the convoluted plots of Elmore Leonard's latest thriller, into one of my old favorites, — *Breakfast at Tiffany's*; *Goodbye, Columbus*; *Our Mutual Friend*; *Wuthering Heights*.

And as it was for me when I was young and surrounded by family, as it is today when I am surrounded by children, reading continues to provide an escape from a crowded house into an imaginary room of one's own.

---

15 Read this quotation from the essay.

> **. . . the women's movement insisted we do something, be something, use our minds as well as our hearts, while in daily life many of us were surrounded by the mundane, the sink full of dishes, car pools, screaming children.**

What does the word "mundane" mean?

A everyday

B exciting

C ones we love

D emotionally-charged

16 Which statement from the essay **best** summarizes the author's main idea?

 F "I began to think that women read differently than men."

 G "And a book provides what it always has: a haven."

 H "We pass on beloved books to our friends. . . ."

 J "Women seem to see reading not only as a solitary activity, but as an opportunity . . ."

17 According to the author, which of the following books would a man **most likely** read?

 A Charles Dickens' *Our Mutual Friend*

 B a biography of Julius Caesar

 C a novel by Anita Bookner

 D Philip Roth's novel, *Goodbye, Columbus*

18 The author says statistics are "slippery things." This is an example of

 F foreshadowing   **H** a metaphor

 G a flashback   **J** alliteration

19 The author writes of "overturned glasses of milk, of toys on the floor, of hours from sunrise to sunset that were horribly busy…" With this description, the author creates feelings of

 A disorder and boredom   **C** excitement and adventure

 B happiness and moderation   **D** order and contentment

20 The author appears to write from the point of view of someone who

 F dislikes reading

 G owns a small book store

 H participated in the civil rights movement

 J is concerned with women's issues

21 The information in the essay would be most useful to someone studying

 A how men and women differ in their work habits

 B how the Internet has affected book sales

 C why women read more books than men

 D why some people prefer television to reading books

Read the poem by Will Allen Droomgoole. Then answer questions 22 through 26.

THE BRIDGE BUILDER

An old man, going a lone highway,
Came, at the evening, cold and gray,
To a chasm, vast and deep, and wide,
Through which was flowing a sullen tide,
The old man crossed in the twilight dim;
The sullen stream had no fears for him;
But he turned, when safe on the other side,
And built a bridge to span the tide.

"Old man," said a fellow pilgrim, near,
"You are wasting strength with building here;
Your journey will end with the ending day;
You never again must pass this way;
You have crossed the chasm, deep and wide —
Why build you the bridge at the eventide?"

The builder lifted his old gray head:
"Good friend, in the path I have come," he said,
"There followeth after me today
A youth, whose feet must pass this way.

This chasm, that has been naught to me,
To that fair-haired youth may a pitfall be.
He, too, must cross in the twilight dim;
Good friend, I am building the bridge for *him*."

Will Allen Droomgoole

22   Which **best** expresses the main theme of the poem?

  F   We must build bridges to understand others better.
  G   We should act to make the world better for others.
  H   We must all act together to protect the natural environment.
  J   We should never overlook the contributions of people in their old age.

23   What does the second stanza (lines 9–14) reveal about the character of the "fellow pilgrim"?

  A   The pilgrim worries about later travelers.
  B   The pilgrim is an experienced carpenter.
  C   The pilgrim thinks more about himself than others.
  D   The pilgrim is concerned about the old man's health.

24   The poem is told from the point of view of

  F   a third-person narrator
  G   the bridge builder
  H   a later traveler
  J   a fellow pilgrim

25   What best describes the tone of this poem?

  A   angry
  B   reflective
  C   persuasive
  D   humorous

26   Read this line from the poem.

  The sullen stream had no fears for him.

  Which literary technique does the poet use in this line?

  F   flashback
  G   simile
  H   alliteration
  J   rhyme

STOP

END OF SESSION 1

SESSION 2

Directions. In this part of the test, you will listen to an article called "The Story of Hook and Loop," which will be read to you twice. The article can be found in the **Teacher's Guide** that accompanies this book. As you listen, you should take notes. You may use these notes to answer the questions that follow. Then you will answer some questions to show how well you have understood what was read.

This test will ask you to write about what you have listened to or read. Your writing will NOT be scored on your personal opinions. It WILL be scored on:

- how clearly you organize and express your ideas
- how accurately and completely you answer the questions
- how well you support your ideas with examples
- how interesting and enjoyable your writing is
- how correctly you use grammar, spelling, punctuation, and paragraphs

---

Whenever you see this symbol, be sure to plan and check your writing.

27 Based on the information from the article, explain how George de Mestral came up with the idea for Velcro. Use details from the article to support your answer.

28 Based on information in the article, explain one obstacle George de Mestral had to overcome to become a successful manufacturer. Use details from the article to support your answer.

29 Using information from the article, list three uses of Velcro in the chart below.

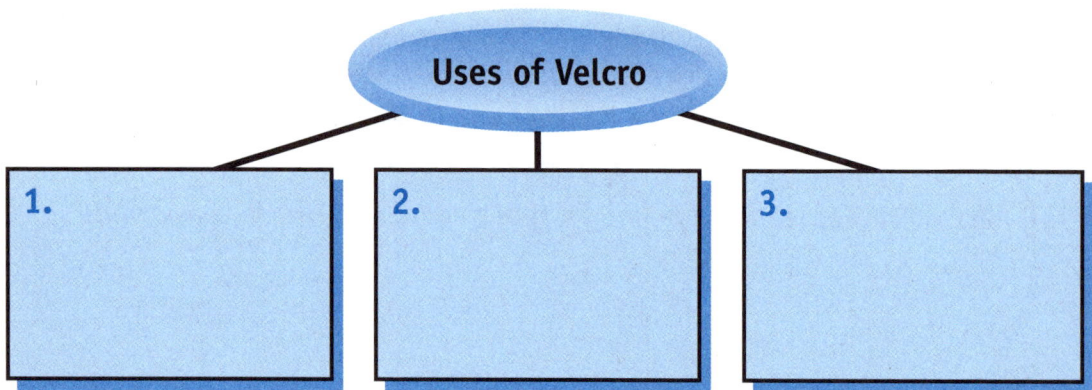

Uses of Velcro

1.

2.

3.

30 George de Mestral is often admired for his inventiveness. Write an essay in which you explain how he was inventive. Use details from the article to support your answer.

In your answer, be sure to

• explain what it means to be "inventive"
• explain how George de Mestral was inventive
• use details from the article to support your answer

Check your writing for correct spelling, grammar, and punctuation.

STOP

END OF SESSION 2

SESSION 3

Directions: In this part of the test, you will read an excerpt from Russell Baker's autobiography *Growing Up* and an excerpt from the novel *The Grapes of Wrath* by John Steinbeck. Both passages tell about the Great Depression, a huge economic downturn in the 1930s in which millions of Americans lost their jobs, savings and homes. You will then answer questions and write about what you have read. You can look back at the two excerpts as often as you like.

GROWING UP
By Russell Baker

I was just a young boy when we moved to Baltimore during the Great Depression. My paper route earned me three dollars a week, sometimes four, and my mother, in addition to her commissions on magazine sales, also had her monthly check from Uncle Willie, but we'd been in Baltimore a year before I knew how desperate things were for her. One Saturday morning she told me she'd need Doris and me to go with her to pick up some food. I had a small wagon she'd bought me to make it easier to move the Sunday papers, and she said I'd better bring it. The three of us set off, passing the grocery store we usually shopped at, and kept walking until we came to a grim street of poverty in the heart of East Baltimore.

"This is where we go," she said when we reached the corner of Fremont and Fayette Street. It looked like a grocery, with big plate-glass windows and people lugging out cardboard cartoons and bulging bags, but it wasn't. I knew very well what it was. "Are we going on relief?" I asked her.

Relief = government assistance similar to welfare today

"Don't ask questions about things you don't know about," she said. "Bring that wagon inside."

I did, and watched with a mixture of shame and greed while men filled

CONTINUED ▶

it with food. None of it was food I liked. There were huge cans of grapefruit juice, paper sacks of cornmeal, bags of rice and prunes. It was hard to believe all this was ours for no money at all, even though none of it was very appetizing.

My wonder at this free bounty quickly changed to embarrassment as we headed home with it. Being on relief was a shameful thing. People who accepted the government's handouts were scorned by everyone I knew as idle no-accounts without enough self respect to pay their own way in the world. I'd often heard my mother say the same thing of families in the neighborhood suspected of being on relief. These, I'd been taught to believe, were people beyond hope. Now we were as low as they were.

Pulling the wagon back toward Lombard Street, with Doris following behind to keep the edible proof of our disgrace from falling off, I knew my mother was far worse off than I'd suspected. She'd never have accepted such shame otherwise. I studied her as she walked along, head high as always, not a bit bowed in disgrace, moving at her usual quick pace. If she'd given up on life, she didn't show it, but on the other hand she was unhappy about something. I dared to mention the dreaded words only once on that trip home.

"Are we on relief now, Mom?"

"Let me worry about that," she said.

What worried me most as we neared home was the possibility we'd be seen with the incriminating food by somebody we knew. There was no mistaking government-surplus food. The grapefruit-juice cans, the prunes and rice, the cornmeal — all were ostentatiously* unlabeled, thus advertising themselves as "government handouts." Everybody in the neighborhood could read them, and our humiliation would be gossiped through every parlor by sundown. I had an inspiration.

"It's hot pulling this wagon," I said. "I'm going to take my sweater off." It wasn't hot, it was on the cool side, but after removing the sweater I laid it across the groceries in the wagon. It wasn't a very effective cover, but my mother was suddenly affected by the heat too.

* prominently

CONTINUED

"It is warm, isn't it, Buddy?" she said. Removing her topcoat, she draped it over the groceries, providing total concealment.

"You want to take your coat off, Doris?" asked my mother.

"I'm not hot, I'm chilly," Doris said.

It didn't matter. My mother's coat was enough to get us home without being exposed as three of life's failures.

31 In the chart below, write the reason why each object is significant to the author. Use details from *Growing Up* to support your answer.

Object	Significance
1 The building on the corner of Fremont and Fayette Street	
2 Unlabeled cans of food	
3 The author's sweater	

32 Explain how the author feels about receiving government relief. Use details from the passage to support your answer.

_____

_____

_____

_____

_____

The *Grapes of Wrath* describes Oklahoma families who lost their farms during the Great Depression. They migrated to California where they lived in tents and became day laborers. The following excerpt describes how these migrants survived California's winter rains. Some of the sentences are in "Okie" dialect (speech pattern).

THE GRAPES OF WRATH
By John Steinbeck

When the first rain started, the migrant people huddled in their tents, saying, It'll soon be over, and asking How long's it likely to go on? And when the puddles formed, the men went out in the rain with shovels and built little dikes around the tents. The beating rain worked at the canvas until it penetrated and sent streams down. And then the little dikes washed out and the water came inside, and the streams wet the beds and blankets. The people sat in wet clothes. They set up boxes and put planks on the boxes. Then, day and night, they sat on the planks.

Migrant camp under eucalyptus trees.

From Security Administration

Besides the tents the old cars stood, and water fouled the ignition wires and water fouled the carburetors. The little gray tents stood in lakes. And at last the people had to move. Then the cars wouldn't start because the wires were shorted; and if the engines would run, deep mud engulfed the wheels. And the people waded away, carrying their wet blankets in their arms. They splashed along, carrying the children, carrying the very old, in their arms. And if a barn stood on high ground, it was filled with people, shivering and hopeless.

Then some went to the relief offices (state welfare offices), and they came sadly back to their own people.

They's rules — you got to be here a year before you can git relief. They say the gov'ment is gonna help. They don' know when.

And gradually the greatest terror of all came along.

They ain't gonna be no kinda work for three months.

CONTINUED

In the barns, the people sat huddled together; and the terror came over them, and their faces were gray with terror. The children cried with hunger, and there was no food. Then the sickness came, pneumonia and measles that went to the eyes and to the mastoids. And the rain fell steadily, and the water flowed over the highways, for the culverts could not carry the water.

Then from the tents, from the crowded barns, groups of sodden men went out, their clothes slopping rags, their shoes muddy pulp. They splashed out through the water, to the towns, to the country stores, to the relief offices, to beg for food, to cringe and beg for food, to beg for relief, to try to steal, to lie. And under the begging, and under the cringing, a hopeless anger began to smolder. And in the little towns pity for the sodden men changed to anger, and anger at the hungry people changed to fear of them. Then sheriffs swore in deputies in droves, and orders were rushed for rifles, for tear gas, for ammunition. Then the hungry men crowded the alleys behind the stores to beg for bread, to beg for rotting vegetables, to steal when they could.

Frantic men pounded on the doors of the doctors; and the doctors were busy. And sad men left word at country stores for the coroner[1] to send a car. The coroners were not too busy. The coroners' wagons backed up through the mud and took out the dead.

Wife and child of migrant worker camping in the Sacramento Valley, 1936.

And the rain pattered relentlessly down, and the streams broke their banks and spread out over the country. Huddled under sheds, lying in wet hay, the hunger and the fear bred anger. Then boys went out, not to beg, but to steal; and men went out weakly, to try to steal.

The sheriffs swore in new deputies and ordered new rifles; and the comfortable people in tight houses felt pity at first, and then distaste, and finally hatred for the migrant people...

The rain stopped. On the fields the water stood, reflecting the gray sky, and the land whispered with moving water. And the men came out of the barns, out of the sheds. They squatted on their hams[2] and looked out over the flood land. And they were silent. And sometimes they talked very quietly. No work till spring. No work. And if no work — no money, no food.

---

[1]Coroner–official who investigates deaths
[2]hams–hamstring tendons in the back of the knee

CONTINUED

Fella had a team of horses, had to use 'em to plow an' cultivate and mow, wouldn' think a turnin' 'em out to starve when they wasn't workin'.

Them's horses — we're men.

The women watched the men, watched to see whether the break[3] had come at last. The women stood silently and watched. And where a number of men gathered together, the fear went from their faces, and anger took its place. And the women sighed with relief for they knew it was all right — the break had not come; the break would never come as long as fear could turn to wrath[4].

_____

[3]break–an emotional breakdown
[4]wrath–anger

33   Explain why the migrant farm workers became angry. Use details in the excerpt from *The Grapes of Wrath* to support your answer.

34   The young Russell Baker and the migrant workers described by John Steinbeck in his novel both suffered during the Great Depression. Write an essay in which you compare their experiences and how they coped with their situations.

In your answer, be sure to

- describe the experiences of Russell Baker and the migrant workers in the Great Depression
- explain how Russell Baker and the migrant workers coped with their situations
- use details from both excerpts to support your answer

Check your writing for correct spelling, grammar, and punctuation.

APPENDIX

This **Appendix** consists of four parts: (1) *Writing Mechanics*; (2) the *5-point Rubric* for scoring short and extended responses; (3) *Listening Passages* referred to in the book; and (4) a **Concept Map of Skills** covered in Session 1.

WRITING MECHANICS

English has rules for standard spelling, capitalization, punctuation, usage, sentence structure and paragraphing. Your extended responses will receive a separate score for how well you follow these rules. This first part of the **Appendix** reviews the major rules in those areas where students most often make mistakes.

SPELLING

Many English words are borrowed from foreign languages with different spelling rules. As a result, you have to memorize the spelling of many words. Even so, there are some general rules that can help you to spell correctly:

★ **Words with *ei* and *ie*.** In general, use *i* before *e*, except after *c*, or when sounding like *ay*, as in **neighbor** or **weigh**. Some words that follow this rule include **receive**, **piece**, **chief**, **believe**, and **shield**. However, there are some exceptions to the rule, such as **weird** and **seize**.

★ **Words with *ght*.** Some words end with *ght* to make the sound *t*. Do not confuse their spelling — **eight**, **night**, **height**, and **weight**.

★ **Silent *e*.** Many English words end in a silent *e*, especially when the sound of the preceding vowel is "long" (says its name): flam*e*, estimat*e*, irritat*e*, despit*e*, compromis*e*.

★ **Double Consonants.** Many words with double consonants were formed by adding a suffix or prefix to the root word. The double consonant indicates the same sound is heard in both syllables.

crammed	unnatural	misspelled	begging
hidden	manned	saddened	fitting

★ **Words with *ph*.** Words with *ph* make an *f* sound.

photography	biogra**ph**y	trium**ph**

★ **Changing the final *y* to *i*.** When a noun ends in *y* after a consonant, change the *y* to *i* and add *es* to make it plural. For example:

story ➜ stories   city ➜ cities   memory ➜ memories

★ **Dropping the final *e*.** When a noun ends in a consonant plus an *e,* drop the final *e* before adding *ing.* For example:

hide ➜ hiding   love ➜ loving   make ➜ making

★ **Plural of nouns ending with *f*.** If a noun ends in *f,* change the *f* to *v* and then add *es* to make it plural. For example:

wolf ➜ wolves   shelf ➜ shelves   elf ➜ elves

★ **Words ending in a consonant.** When you want to add *ing, ed,* or *er* to a word that ends in a single consonant, double the last letter — *planning, planned,* or *planner.* This does not apply to most words ending in *w, x,* or *y.* For example: *blowing, taxed,* or *player.*

CAPITALIZATION

There are several important rules you should know for when to capitalize a word.

★ Always capitalize the pronoun *I*.

★ Always begin the first word of each sentence with a capital letter:

He likes strawberry milkshakes.

★ **Proper Nouns** are capitalized. A **proper noun** names a specific person, place or thing. For example, the word *forest* is not a proper noun, since there are many forests. However, *Sherwood Forest* is a proper noun, since it is the name of a particular forest. Other examples of proper nouns are:

- **Names of Streets:** *Broadway, Fifth Avenue, First Street*
- **Towns and Cities:** *Merrick, Albany, Syracuse*
- **Names of Countries:** *China, Canada, Mexico*
- **Names of People:** *Tim, Ralph, Britney*
- **Days of the Week:** *Monday, Thursday, Sunday*
- **Holidays:** *Thanksgiving, New Year's Day, Halloween*

★ **Proper Adjectives.** Adjectives made out of proper nouns are capitalized: *Chinese food, French pastry*

PUNCTUATION

Here are some rules you should know for punctuation:

★ Use **commas** to separate the items in a list, in dates, in quotations, and in any places in a sentence where you would pause. Also use commas to separate a city from its state or country:

*Lenny brought tomatoes, eggs, milk, and a
loaf of bread to his hotel room in Syracuse, New York.*

★ Use commas before *and*, *or*, and *but* in compound sentences:

Katy refused to listen, but I insisted that she leave.

★ Use periods at the end of abbreviations: *Mr., Ms., Mrs., U.S.A.*

★ Use apostrophes to show possession or contractions:

Jack's boat   I'm = I am

★ Use quotation marks for direct speech: *"I want to go home," she said.*

★ Always end a sentence with a *period*, *question mark* or *exclamation point*.

- End statements with a period: *The monkey ate a bunch of bananas.*
- End questions with a question mark: *What time is it?*
- End sentences that show strong feelings, such as surprise or laughter, with an exclamation point: *That hat looks so silly on you!*

USAGE

You should be familiar with the correct use of different parts of speech, such as pronouns, verbs, adjectives, and adverbs.

PRONOUNS

A **pronoun** takes the place of a noun used earlier in a speech or writing. The earlier noun is known as the **antecedent**. When a pronoun is used, it must be clear what antecedent the pronoun is replacing.

★ The most common pronouns are *I, we, you, he, she, it,* and *they*. These **subject pronouns** can be used as the subject of a sentence: *"He liked candy."*

★ Sometimes the pronoun is the object of a sentence or of a prepositional phrase. The most common **object pronouns** are *me, us, you, him, her, it,* and *them*.

> Rachel loved to eat *pancakes*. She ate *them* almost every day.

★ Pronouns can also show ownership or possession. The most important **possessive pronouns** are *my, your, his, her, its, our, your,* and *their*.

> *Jason* played in the yard. His mother watched from *her* window.

★ A pronoun must agree with its antecedent in *number* (*singular/plural*) and *gender* (*male/female*). For example, the pronoun must be singular if it replaces a singular antecedent. Remember that **each, anyone, everyone, everybody, nobody,** and **somebody** are singular and take singular pronouns:

> *"**Each** player grabbed **his** baseball mitt."*

TROUBLESOME PRONOUNS

★ *It's* is a contraction for *it is*. *Its* without an apostrophe shows possession.
  • *It's time for you to return the bicycle to its owner."*

★ *There — their — they're*
  • *There* is for a place: *"It is over there."*
  • *Their* shows possession: *"**Their** taxi is waiting."*
  • *They're* is a contraction for *they are*: *"**They're** ready to leave."*

★ *Who, Whom, Whose, Who's*
  • *Who* is used as the subject of a sentence or clause. *"**Who** is that?"*
  • *Whom* is used in written English as the object of a sentence, clause, or preposition. *"**Whom** did she see?"*
  • *Whose* is a possessive referring to ownership: *"**Whose** is that?"*
  • *Who's* is a contraction for *who is*: *"**Who's** that?"* (*Who is that?*)

VERBS

Verbs tell us what nouns do or what is being done to them. For example, action verbs like *walk, jump,* and *run* tell what the subject of a sentence does. Linking verbs, like *to be*, do not express action but link the subject to an adjective or another noun. They tell how the subject is, seems, or feels: She *is* happy.

⭐ The tense of a verb tells us whether an action happens in the past, present or future. Make sure to keep your tenses consistent. If you are telling a story in the past tense, keep all the verbs used in the story in the past tense.

- To make the present tense of most verbs, add *s* if the subject is singular. "*Fran **likes** school.* Use the plain form of the verb for plural subjects and with the singular pronouns *I* and *You*: *Her brothers **like** vacations.*"

- To make the past tense of most verbs, add *ed*. For example:
  "*Dinosaurs once **lived** in this area.*"

- Many common verbs take an irregular form in the past tense:

Present Tense	Past Tense
give	gave
get	got

- To make the future tense of most verbs, use ***will*** or ***is going to*** in front of the plain form of the verb. For example: "*José **will leave** soon.*"

ADJECTIVES

Adjectives describe or modify nouns. They usually go before a noun: "*The **pretty** girl walked away.*" Predicate adjectives follow a linking verb: "*She is **pretty**.*"

⭐ Most action verbs can be turned into adjectives by adding ***ing***: *laughing, running, smiling*. Proper nouns can often be turned into proper adjectives, which are also capitalized. For example: "*She was wearing **Nike** sneakers.*"

⭐ Adjectives can be used to compare people, places, or things.

- To say that one thing is superior to another, add *er* to the adjective:
  "*Jack is taller than Eric.*"

- To say one thing is the most or best out of *more* than two, add *est*:
  "*Adbul is the tallest boy in the class.*"

- For longer adjectives, use ***more*** or ***most*** in comparisons. For example:
  "She was ***more*** intelligent than her sister."

- Never combine ***more*** or ***most*** with *er* or *est*: For example:
  "She was ***more taller*** than her sister" — is clearly wrong.

ADVERBS

Adverbs describe or modify verbs, adjectives, or other adverbs. Adverbs give greater clarity to the action of a sentence. They tell us *where*, *when*, or *how* an action happens.

The green car went *quickly* up the large hill.
Brian *often* goes to the store

★ Many adjectives can be changed into adverbs by adding *ly*

- *quick ———> quickly*
- *slow ———> slowly*

★ *Good* is an adjective, not an adverb. Use *well* as the adverb, but use *good* as a predicate adjective.

- Correct: "*He played well.*"
- Incorrect: "*He played good.*"

SENTENCES

Every **sentence** should express a complete idea and contain a *subject* and a *predicate*. The **subject** is who or what the sentence is about. It may be one or several words. The **predicate** is what the subject does or what happens to the subject in the sentence. It provides the action of the sentence.

SENTENCE FRAGMENTS

A group of words does not make up a sentence if it does not express a complete thought.

★ Clauses beginning with *after*, *until*, *because*, or *since* are not complete sentences by themselves. For example, this is not a sentence:
"After I went shopping."

★ Words ending in *ing* cannot be used as the verb in a sentence without a helping verb. For example, this is not a sentence:
"The girls making a cake."

★ To correct a sentence fragment, you need to complete the thought. Often, you can simply join the sentence fragment to another fragment or another sentence. For example: **"After I went shopping, I went home."**

RUN-ON SENTENCES

The opposite of a sentence fragment is a run-on sentence. A **run-on sentence** usually occurs when the writer joins separate sentences together by commas. For example:

"Nancy liked the summer, her father preferred the fall."

★ There are several ways to correct run-on sentences. One way is to divide the run-on sentence into two or more separate sentences:

"Nancy liked the summer. Her father preferred the fall."

★ A second approach is to turn the run-on sentence into a *compound* sentence by adding **and**, **but** or **or**:

"Nancy liked the summer, but her father preferred the fall."

★ You may also be able to create a complex sentence by adding **that**, **which**, **who**, **since**, **because**, **while** or **as**:

"Nancy liked the summer, while her father preferred the fall."

SUBJECT-VERB AGREEMENT

A very common mistake in sentences often occurs in *subject / verb agreement*. The noun (*subject*) and verb (*predicate*) of the sentence must agree in number.

★ A **singular subject** refers to **one** person, place or thing. If the subject of a sentence is singular, you must use a verb in its **singular form.**

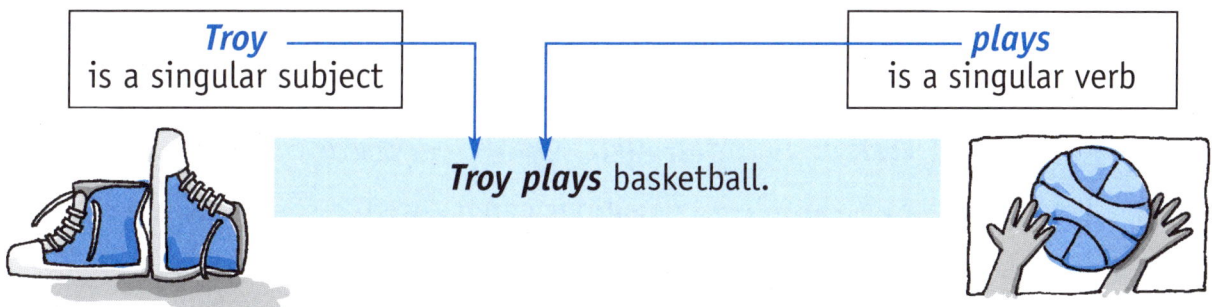

Troy is a singular subject		*plays* is a singular verb

Troy plays basketball.

★ A **plural subject** consists of **more than one** person, place, or thing. The subject may be a plural noun (*children*) or a compound subject (*Jim and Jack*). If the subject of a sentence is plural, the verb must be in its plural form.

Jack *likes* to drink water.
Jim and Jack *like* to drink water.
The children *like* to drink water.

★   A prepositional phrase is **never** part of the subject. A singular subject followed by a prepositional phrase therefore takes a singular verb.

The man with his sisters enjoys going to the movies

PARAGRAPHS

A **paragraph** is a group of sentences on the same topic. Often, a paragraph has a topic sentence identifying what it is about.

★   If you are changing your topic, you should begin a new paragraph. Do not mix several different subjects in the same paragraph.

★   Each new paragraph should begin on a new line and be **indented**.

TRANSITIONS

Transitional words and phrases link together different ideas by explaining the relationship between them. They act as signposts telling readers they are entering a new area or topic in your writing. By using transitions, your writing will flow more smoothly.

★   **Time and Place.** Some transitions indicates a change in time or place:
  He ate dinner at 7 o'clock. Later that evening, he went to bed.

  While and *meanwhile* indicate a change of place at the same time:
  Tom was working in Manhattan, while Cheryl was in Albany.

★   **New Points or Examples.** Transitions can be used to show you are moving from one point to the next:
  A second reason for inspecting luggage at airports is to stop people from taking weapons on airplanes.

★   **Introducing Differences.** Transitions often introduce something that is different from or contrary to what has already been said. *However*, *on the other hand*, *nevertheless*, *but*, and *although* mark a contrast or change in direction:
  I enjoy jogging. However, in the summer heat I prefer to swim.

★   **Conclusions.** Transitions can be used to introduce a conclusion:
  Therefore, he had no choice but to help his father.

SCORING RUBRIC

Your short responses and extended response will be scored together for Session 2 and Session 3. The following shows New York State's scoring rubric for each point value from 0 to 5 points.

5 POINTS

Taken as a whole, the responses
- fulfill the requirements of the tasks
- address the theme or key elements of the text
- show a thorough interpretation of the text
- make some connections beyond the text
- develop ideas fully with thorough elaboration
- make effective use of relevant and accurate examples from the text

In addition, the extended response
- establishes and maintains a clear focus
- shows a logical sequence of ideas through the use of appropriate transitions or other devices
- is fluent and easy to read, with a sense of engagement or voice
- uses varied sentence structures and some above-grade-level vocabulary

4 POINTS

Taken as a whole, the responses
- fulfill some requirements of the tasks
- address some key elements of the text
- show a predominantly literal interpretation of the text
- make some connections
- may be brief, with little elaboration, but are sufficiently developed to answer the questions
- provide some examples and details from the text
- may include minor inaccuracies

In addition, the extended response
- is generally focused, though may include some irrelevant details
- shows a clear attempt at organization
- is readable, with some sense of engagement or voice
- primarily uses simple sentences and vocabulary

3 POINTS

Taken as a whole, the responses
- fulfill some requirements of the tasks
- address a few key elements of the text
- show some gaps in understanding of the text
- make some connections
- are brief, with little elaboration or development
- provide few examples and details from the text
- may include some minor inaccuracies

In addition, the extended response
- shows an attempt to maintain focus, though may include some tangents
- shows an attempt at organization
- is readable, with some sense of engagement or voice
- primarily uses simple sentences and basic vocabulary

2 POINTS

Taken as a whole, the responses
- fulfill some requirements of the tasks
- address basic elements of the text
- show little evidence that the student understood more than parts of the text
- make few connections
- provide very few text-based examples and details
- may include some inaccurate details

In addition, the extended response
- may show an attempt to establish a focus
- may include some irrelevant information
- shows little attempt at organization
- is readable, with little sense of engagement or voice
- uses minimal vocabulary
- may indicate fragmented thoughts

1 POINT

Taken as a whole, the responses
- fulfill very few requirements of the tasks
- address few elements of the text
- show little evidence that the student understood more than parts of the text
- make little to no connections
- provide almost no text-based examples and details
- may include inaccurate information

In addition, the extended response
- shows little attempt to establish a focus
- may be repetitive, focusing on minor details or irrelevant information
- shows little attempt at organization
- is difficult to read, with little or no sense of engagement or voice
- uses minimal vocabulary
- may indicate fragmented thoughts

0 POINTS

The responses are completely incorrect, irrelevant, or incoherent.

STARTING A NEW LIFE
by Jasmina Hamiclovic

We left our nation of Bosnia because war came to our town. People from neighboring Serbia invaded and attacked us because we were Muslims. My parents were fired from their jobs, and soldiers took over our house. We soon heard rumors of terrible violence against Bosnian Muslims. This only heightened the fear and terror my parents were feeling.

My family then fled to our cousins in the city of Zagreb. There we learned we had a chance to go to America. In Zagreb they had *E.R.*, *Baywatch*, and *General Hospital* with subtitles. I tried to learn English by watching these American television programs. I was kind of happy and kind of sad to hear we were going to America. We took a long bus ride, then five or six airplanes, to get to San Francisco.

Using a new language was the biggest difference I faced in the United States. There were other differences as well. I liked my new school, but at the beginning it was kind of weird. Kids have such a different attitude here. They would not listen to the teacher. At home in Bosnia, if the teacher says, "Sit down," kids sit down. Not here. American kids might answer, "Shut up!" No wonder my new teachers said I was polite and respectful.

In Bosnia, I had heard that people in America kidnap kids. At first, I was scared of going to school alone, and scared of playing alone. Then I saw that when I go to school, no one follows me, and I got over it. Now I know that America is safer than I thought.

I still miss my old school, friends, teachers, and river where I used to go swimming. But I am glad we came here. Here in San Francisco there are four thousand people from my country. We are Muslim and celebrate our holidays together. We are safe from the violence in our home country, and have the chance to make new friends.

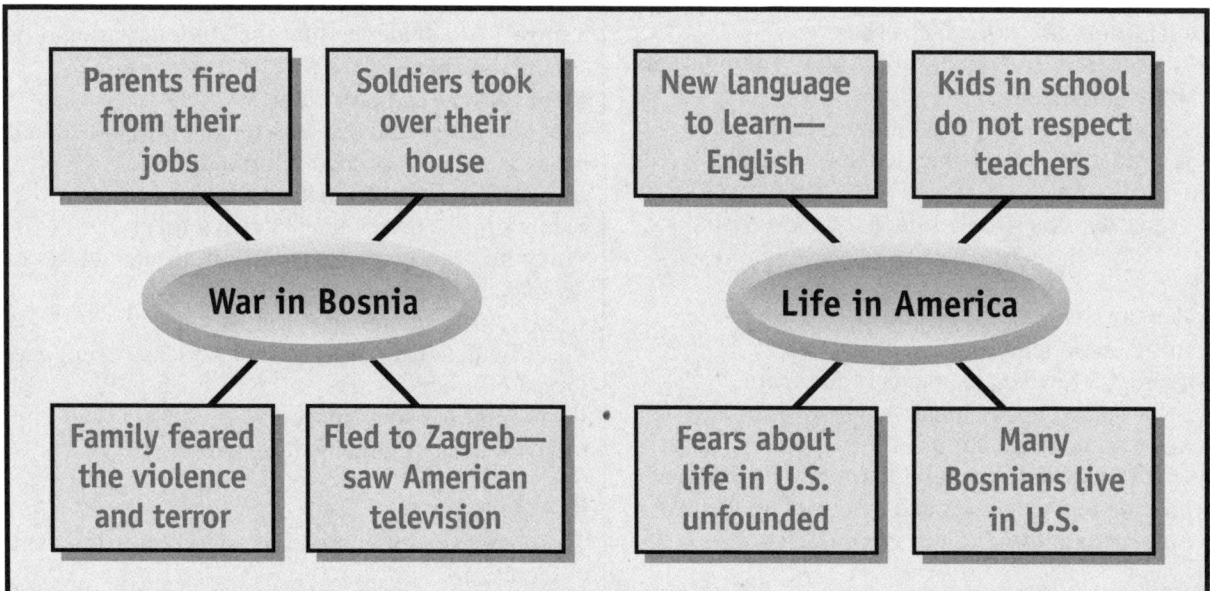

Parents fired from their jobs	Soldiers took over their house	New language to learn— English	Kids in school do not respect teachers

War in Bosnia   **Life in America**

Family feared the violence and terror	Fled to Zagreb— saw American television	Fears about life in U.S. unfounded	Many Bosnians live in U.S.

KEEPING TIME IN A TIMELESS PLACE

Three hundred years ago, Versailles (Ver' sī) was the magnificent palace of King Louis XIV of France. Today, it is not just a museum, but a national treasure.

Once a week, Bernard Draux joins the secret life of Versailles, a palace where even without its long-gone kings much still happens. Mr. Draux is Versailles' official clockmaker and timekeeper. His task is to wind and repair close to 100 antique clocks that once served Europe's most glittering court. Every Monday, when Versailles is closed, he sets out on his solitary mission with a small set of precision tools and a bundle of keys.

There are gold-covered clocks, fixed into bronze camels or marble elephants. Some have music boxes hidden inside. Grand 18th-century pieces, which have survived theft and revolution, record not just the hour, date and month but also the movements of the planets.

Why, Mr. Draux was asked, was such an effort being made to record the time in such a timeless place? "The clocks belong here," he said. "They must preserve their beauty and they must work properly. It looks bad when clocks fail to keep the right time."

"Each clock is unique because it is made like a work of art, before the age of mass production," Daux murmured. "Each is different, I don't really know a clock until I have taken it apart. And of course, there are never instructions."

Mr. Draux's task may be one of a kind, but it offers a glimpse of the enormous energy and cost that France puts into preserving its great treasures and museums. France gives much weight to traditional skills, even as it adopts its share of American-style mass-produced goods. The government employs thousands of men and women at carving antique wood or stone, repairing stucco or wrought iron, or fixing yards of ancient frames and weavings. Such trades, and the unfashionable patience they require, may gain little public applause elsewhere, but here they rank as high as patriotism. Many French believe these trades are their national cultural identity. They see a need to preserve French uniqueness and distinctiveness. They warn that globalized manufacture and trade, if left uncontrolled, may end up covering the world with a blanket of sameness.

Investing in history has its rewards. As one of the world's main tourist destinations, Versailles is visited by 10 million people a year. The palace, with its 700 rooms and thousands of windows, statues, and chandeliers, has been high maintenance ever since the 1660s when Louis XIV first moved in. Today's staff of 900 looks after it, although hundreds more are now involved in the museum's most ambitious renovation project. The overhaul is expected to take 17 years and to cost more than $450 million. Mr. Draux hopes that the restoration will include some of the exceptional clocks that are in storage, awaiting repair.

Clocks may not loom large in the lore about the extravagance of the royalty here, but by many accounts there was little free time. "Clocks were very important in the 17th century because court life was full of rigor and rituals," says one French historian. "There were fixed times for the rising of the king, for prayers, for government meetings, for meals, for walks, for the hunt, for concerts and so on. Everyone had to be on their toes. Louis XIV had not one, but four clockmakers working for him," he said. "When the king traveled, the clockmakers and many clocks went with him."

This concept map shows the reading comprehinsion skills you learned in **Session 1** of this book. Each skill is related to a question type found on the **Grade 8 English Language Arts Test**. Review the relevant chapter if you can't remember that skill.

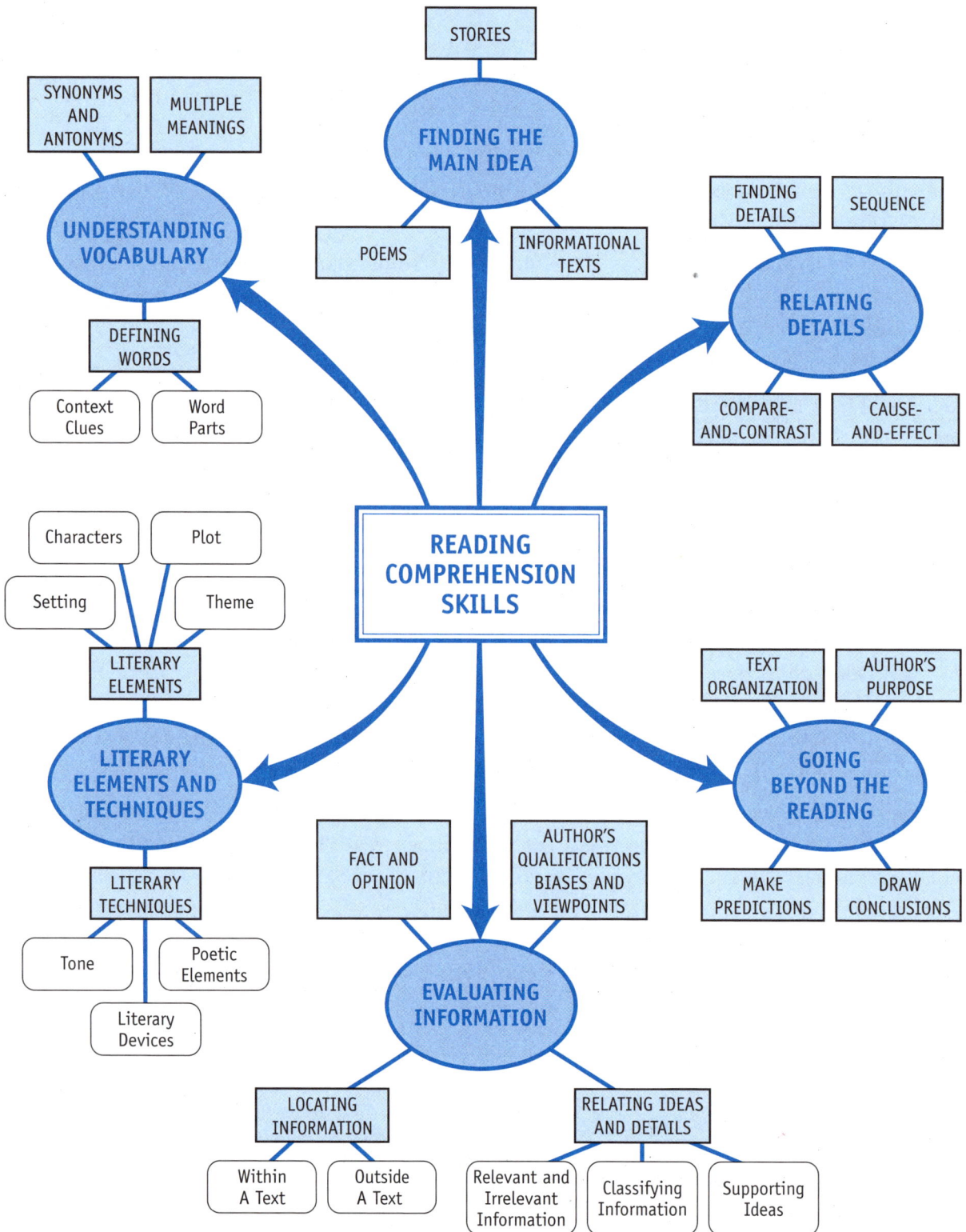

STORIES

FINDING THE MAIN IDEA

POEMS

INFORMATIONAL TEXTS

SYNONYMS AND ANTONYMS

MULTIPLE MEANINGS

UNDERSTANDING VOCABULARY

DEFINING WORDS

Context Clues

Word Parts

FINDING DETAILS

SEQUENCE

RELATING DETAILS

COMPARE-AND-CONTRAST

CAUSE-AND-EFFECT

Characters

Plot

Setting

Theme

LITERARY ELEMENTS

READING COMPREHENSION SKILLS

LITERARY ELEMENTS AND TECHNIQUES

LITERARY TECHNIQUES

Tone

Poetic Elements

Literary Devices

FACT AND OPINION

AUTHOR'S QUALIFICATIONS BIASES AND VIEWPOINTS

EVALUATING INFORMATION

LOCATING INFORMATION

Within A Text

Outside A Text

RELATING IDEAS AND DETAILS

Relevant and Irrelevant Information

Classifying Information

Supporting Ideas

TEXT ORGANIZATION

AUTHOR'S PURPOSE

GOING BEYOND THE READING

MAKE PREDICTIONS

DRAW CONCLUSIONS